The Pocket Encyclopaedia of

BRITISH
STEAM LOCOMOTIVES
IN COLOUR

by
O. S. NOCK
B.Sc., M.I.C.E., M.I. Mech E., M.I. Loco E.

With 192 locomotives illustrated by
CLIFFORD and WENDY MEADWAY

LONDON
BLANDFORD PRESS

© 1964 Blandford Press Ltd.
167 High Holborn, London WC1V 6PH
Second impression 1966
Third impression 1968
Fourth impression 1973

ISBN 0 7137 0350 4

Made in Great Britain
Colour illustrations printed in photogravure
by D. H. Greaves Limited, Scarborough, Yorkshire
on Bowaters Bladecote paper,
and text printed and books bound
by Richard Clay (The Chaucer Press), Ltd.,
Bungay, Suffolk

CONTENTS

MAPS

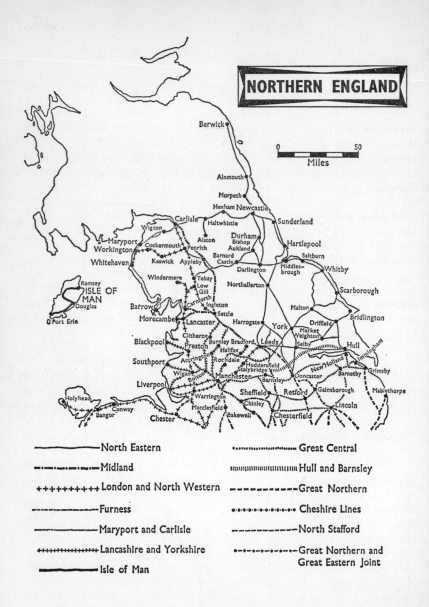

NORTHERN ENGLAND

0 ____ 50
Miles

Berwick

Alnmouth

Morpeth

Hexham Newcastle

Carlisle Haltwhistle Sunderland

Wigton Durham
Alston Bishop Hartlepool
Maryport Cockermouth Penrith Aukland
Workington Keswick Appleby Barnard Saltburn
Whitehaven Castle Darlington Middles- Whitby
Windermere brough

Tebay Northallerton Scarborough
Barrow Low Malton
ISLE OF Gill Bridlington
Ramsey MAN Carnforth Ingleton Driffield
Douglas Morecambe Settle York Market
Port Erin Lancaster Harrogate Weighton
Clitheroe Bradford Selby Hull
Blackpool Preston Burnley Leeds Immingham
Halifax New Holland
Accrington Rochdale Huddersfield Grimsby
Southport Wigan Stalybridge Doncaster Barnetby
Bolton Manchester Barnsley Mablethorpe
Liverpool Warrington Sheffield Retford Gainsborough
Holyhead Macclesfield Chinley Lincoln
Bangor Conway Bakewell Chesterfield
Chester

————— North Eastern	•••••••••••••••• Great Central
—··—··—··— Midland	ⅲⅲⅲⅲⅲⅲⅲⅲ Hull and Barnsley
+++++++++ London and North Western	————— Great Northern
——————— Furness	•••••••••• Cheshire Lines
————— Maryport and Carlisle	————— North Stafford
++++++++++ Lancashire and Yorkshire	•—·—·—·—·— Great Northern and
▬▬▬▬ Isle of Man	Great Eastern Joint

4

PREFACE

When the idea of a book illustrating, in full colour, some 200 different locomotives was first put to me I must admit I was incredulous. The prospect seemed too near the railway enthusiast's conception of Valhalla to be true! But my friends of the Blandford Press showed me some beautiful volumes they had already produced in the same series, at a price within the pocket of the humblest of enthusiasts, and I listened to the production programme outlined to me with a quickened interest. Still there remained the question of the pictures. As the book was intended to cover the entire history of the British steam locomotive photographs were out of the question. One hundred and ninety-two pictures had got to be *painted*! It was then that I was introduced to Charles Rickitt and his Portman Artists. Still incredulous I chose a subject for a trial picture, but when I saw the result my doubts vanished, and the only problem that remained was that of getting the remaining 191 finished in time to meet the production schedule.

The only problem! There were many facets to it. The mere job of choosing the subjects – only 192 from the thousands of different locomotives that have run in Great Britain since the opening of the Stockton and Darlington Railway – was baffling at times, and embarrassing. Some claimants among the earlier subjects had to be discarded; information about their colour and finish was non-existent. But from the very outset I enjoyed the happiest of collaborations with Charles Rickitt, and with his artists Cliff and Wendy Meadway. From the first day, when we picnicked amid photographs, files, reference books and goodness knows what else in my home, locomotives have been painted with a speed and accuracy that could be likened to the production line of a modern factory. What might have been a nerve-racking race against time has been a great pleasure: sending the Meadways subject after subject in rapid succession, and seeing the results so swiftly and beautifully rendered.

In preparing the plates, we have made frequent reference to the well-established sources of historical railway information: to the Science Museum, London; to the Transport Museum at Clapham; and the railway museums at York and Swindon; to the files of 'The Locomotive Magazine'. For information upon certain specific liveries I am indebted to Mr John S. McLean, Mr Harold Chase, and to Mr Ivo Peters.

In points of detail, there may be readers who will feel that some locomotives might well have been left out, to make room for others of their own fancy. Partisanship for one or other of the pre-grouping companies certainly runs to fever heat at times, though not quite to the extent jocularly suggested by one of my closest railway friends. On telling him how carefully I had striven to try and give the fairest distribution among the companies he said: 'Oh well, if you've given 70 per cent to the Great Western and 30 per cent to the rest if would be about right'!

Our aim has been to provide the broadest possible picture of steam locomotive history. For that reason it has been impossible to include certain isolated 'specials', as when the London and North Western Railway painted one large express locomotive in pillar-box red and another in *white*, to celebrate the Diamond Jubilee of Queen Victoria's reign; or when the engines set aside for hauling the Queen's Messenger trains between Aberdeen and Ballater were painted in Royal Stewart tartan. Another livery that is missing is the short-lived 'silver' of the first L.N.E.R. streamlined 'A4' Pacific engines. No more than one picture could be allocated to each engine design, and as it was in the Garter Blue that the 'A4s' achieved their greatest fame, so it is in this style that the immortal *Mallard* is depicted.

As always, I have had invaluable help from Olivia, my wife. She too has her tastes in locomotive design, and in her view all single-wheelers not having slotted splashers should have been excluded! To her, as typist, art-critic and hostess to my collaborators, my best thanks are due.

Silver Cedars
High Bannerdown
Bath

Brock

March 1964

HISTORICAL INTRODUCTION

RAILWAYS in a number of crude forms had existed for many years before the birth of George Stephenson. By putting the primitive wagons of the day on to rails instead of trundling them along rough and badly maintained roads it was found that horses could pull far heavier loads, and the Stockton and Darlington Railway, which is generally considered to be the springboard from which the railway system of this country – and the world – originated, was laid out for horse traction. The geography of County Durham aided this general design. The country falls from the coalfields of Bishop Auckland to the sea, and horses could comfortably manage long trains of heavily loaded cauldron wagons, and equally well haul the empties back to the colliery districts. At the opening of the line, however, in 1825, the Company had one steam locomotive, the famous engine that now stands on a pedestal of honour in Darlington station, and in the great vision of development held by George Stephenson she was to be the forerunner of many more.

The *Locomotion*, for such she was named, was far from successful, however, and for many years George Stephenson and his strongest supporters had to fight an uphill battle against those who still favoured horse traction. And while the matter of motive power remained unresolved the rapid development of railways hung fire. The issue was settled beyond doubt by the trials at Rainhill on the line of the Liverpool and Manchester Railway in 1829, when the engine built by George Stephenson's son, Robert, won the prize offered by the directors for the best locomotive that could fulfil certain speed and haulage conditions. This locomotive was the *Rocket*, which more truly than the *Locomotion* of 1825 was the true progenitor of the machine that was to revolutionize inland transport in Great Britain. In the success of steam-worked railways men had both hopes and fears for the future. It was a time of great social unrest and evolution, and while facilitating the flow of commerce, railways would, it was feared, also make easier the movement of radical elements of the population, to spread discontent and trouble for the establishment. This, of course, was to take the narrowest possible view of a movement which, once started, proved to be irresistible.

Railways would have spread in any case, for transport of minerals, and the products of the new industries that were growing up in the country. But it was the steam locomotive that provided the factor that changed the entire life of the country – SPEED.

With speed also developed the capacity for the haulage of heavy loads. The steam locomotive not only provided means for enabling people to travel faster, but it made travel cheap. Simple souls who had never ventured beyond the confines of their own village could now travel at a penny a mile, or even cheaper on special excursion trips. Railways made easier the flow of commerce; merchants could travel easier and faster to see their clients; the day of the 'commercial traveller' was at hand. But perhaps of greater benefit to the country as a whole was the way in which railways, through the haulage capacity of the steam locomotive, brought down the price of consumer goods. An early railway manager was once horrified at the idea of carrying coal; but the opening of the Great Northern Railway, from Doncaster to London, in 1850, showed what could be done. This railway realized that far more revenue was likely to be gained from carrying minerals than passengers and the result of its enterprize and the effectiveness of the powerful locomotives used was so to revolutionize transport that the price of household coal in London was reduced from 30s. a ton to 17s.

The success of steam locomotives in both goods and passenger services led inevitably to greater demands being made upon them. Whereas today some of the greatest engineering brains are concentrated upon the development of nuclear power, electronics and so on, in mid-Victorian times the needs of railways and particularly the steam locomotive were second to none. These needs fostered the development of new engineering processes, in the iron and brass foundries, in heavy forging, and in the manufacture of iron itself. Railway needs led to improvements in technique that came to benefit the trade of the country as a whole. In no field was the development of the use of steel more striking than on railways. The need of something harder and stronger than wrought iron, for wheels, rails, and other moving parts subject to hard wear, fostered the rapid development of steel, and it is remarkable that the very first plant *anywhere in the world* for manufacture of steel on a commercial scale was put into operation at the Crewe locomotive works of the London and North Western Railway, in 1864. It was extensively used, not only for the production of locomotive parts, but to roll the rails they ran upon. By the year 1913 the output of the Crewe steel works had reached 50,000 tons per annum.

The influence of the steam locomotive was something infinitely greater than that of mere speed. Steam traction made travel cheap, easy, and relatively comfortable. While the rich travelled first class, in closed carriages that first resembled the old stage coaches, humbler folk experienced the pleasure of seeing something of the country from the open, third-class 'carriages'. Harrowing pictures have been painted of the miseries of travelling 'third' in those days, and spartan the conditions certainly could be in wet or wintry weather; but early excursion trains, however slow and draughty, were very popular, and undoubtedly contributed to the gradual spread of the broader education of the nineteenth century.

One is entitled to look with some awe and reverence to the unique, self-contained piece of machinery that was indeed the phenomenon of the nineteenth century. From the dawn of history the fastest mode of transport known to man was that of a galloping horse, and yet, within twenty years of the opening of the Stockton and Darlington Railway, there were steam locomotives capable of travelling at 60 m.p.h. By the seventies of last century speeds of 80 m.p.h. were occasionally being touched, and by 1904 a speed of 100 m.p.h. had been attained, on the Great Western Railway.

Inevitably the locomotive became the centrepiece of the entire railway scene. The passengers might be carried in open trucks, and later in roofed affairs that strongly suggested a cavalcade of dog-boxes, but the locomotives were arrayed in a splendour of polished metal and gleaming paint, and their drivers and firemen delighted in keeping them spotless. As the railway network of the country developed, and many of the earlier companies amalgamated to form the great trunk lines the names of which were household words prior to 1923, a series of very famous and beautiful engine liveries became established as standard, and in the colour plates of this book arranged largely, though not strictly, in chronological order one can follow this process of development. Among the larger railways the heights of magnificence were reached in the last years of the nineteenth century, and on such lines as the Great Western, the Midland, the Brighton, the North Eastern, and the Highland the dazzling array could not have been more ornate, yet withal in excellent taste.

In looking at the colour plates in this book one can trace how the quaint machines of the eighteen-thirties gave way to more solid, reliable locomotives. The overall efficiency was not very great, but in mid-Victorian times coal was cheap, and the main thing was to have machines that were inherently reliable. It was around the year 1880 that the sunny climate surrounding railway operation began to change. It is true that there had been lean times in the years following the railway investment mania, and the mid-sixties were a time of severe trade depression. But from 1880 onwards engineers began to seek means of securing greater efficiency in operation, and of reducing the coal bill. In marine engineering double- and triple-expansion engines were by that time commonplace, and many experiments were made with steam locomotives having compound or two-stage expansion of the steam. None of the nineteenth-century experiments in Great Britain had any lasting success – save one, chiefly because compounding brought with it certain gadgets, the ineffectiveness of which far outweighed any increase in thermal efficiency that might have been secured by compound rather than single-stage expansion.

There are pictures of the Webb compounds, built in such large numbers for the London and North Western Railway, at Crewe; there is one of the graceful and gaily adorned Worsdell von Borries compounds built at Gateshead, for the North Eastern Railway. But it was in purchase of a French-built de Glehn compound, the *La France* in 1903, that the Great Western virtually dealt the death-blow to the compound principle in Great Britain. For at Swindon, G. J. Churchward, one of the greatest masters of steam locomotive design, built single-expansion machines that were the superior of the French compounds, and *La France* was a very good compound too. The foundations of the modern engine were laid in those first momentous years of the twentieth century at Swindon, and in time all the railways of Britain were to adopt the principles established in the big Churchward 4-6-0s of the 'Saint' and 'Star' classes.

While these pages record the more spectacular developments in locomotive design they also reflect social history in depicting small tank engines that worked the breadwinners' trains around London. Richly adorned locomotives were not confined to main line expresses, and the tank engines of the North London, the London, Chatham and Dover, and of the Metropolitan, were little masterpieces of the decorative art. Goods engines were not excluded either, and the Stephenson long-boilered goods, used for hauling the coal trains on the Stockton and Darlington section of the North Eastern Railway, must surely rank as one of the most exquisitely painted pieces of machinery of all time.

When it comes to the conveyance of coal the local railways in South Wales have a place of their own. Each of the mining valleys came to have its own railway. Some of these lines were branches of the great trunk concerns like the London and North Western, and the Great Western; but in other of the valleys were to be found stoutly independent local companies like the Taff Vale, the Rhymney, and the Brecon and Merthyr. The faster they carried the coal down to the ports at Cardiff and Newport the faster it was mined at the pits, and eventually the trains of the various companies were virtually queueing up to get alongside the wharves in Cardiff. The coal-owners grew restive; congestion grew rather than lessened, and so a group of enterprising businessmen floated yet another new railway company, the Barry, and soon that line was also carrying coal almost to the limit of its capacity. The engines of the coal-carrying lines were not the least attractive in the zenith of the steam age.

As industry spread, fostered by the facility of rail transport, so the population grew and houses were in great demand. With that demand came a tremendous boom in the slate industry of North Wales. At Blaenau Festiniog the quarries were high in the mountains, and no locomotive power was needed at first to carry the slates down to sea-going ships at Portmadoc. The trains descended by gravity, and horses pulled the empties back to the quarries. But as the trade increased the loads became too much for the horses, and some of the most fascinating little narrow gauge locomotives ever devised – Robert Fairlie's 'double-engines' – were put to work. With the Festiniog came other narrow gauge railways in North Wales, while a classic example of one of these tiny concerns still remains in operation, the Talyllyn.

Railways, as required by British law, were expensive things to build and run where the traffic was light, and in many districts, long before the days of motor cars and lorries, something less pretentious was felt to be necessary. The necessary legislation, providing for numerous relaxations from main line standards, was given by the Light Railway Act of 1896, and a most picturesque line built under these provisions was to be seen in the Leek and Manifold Railway in the Derbyshire hills. Because of the strict limitation of maximum speed a light railway was not required to be fenced, and in consequence one saw, for the only time in England, locomotives with large headlamps to pick out animals or any other obstruction that might be on the rails at night. These narrow gauge lines, like the Lynton and Barnstaple, provided many attractions for the railway connoisseur, but few of them made any money for their owners.

In the twentieth century, on the main lines, the form and styling of locomotives is in some instances a reflection of national affairs. One by one the gay liveries of old began to disappear. Goods engines in ever-increasing numbers began to be painted black, and the onset of the First World War soon witnessed the painting over of much of the polished brass and copper work. The South-Eastern and Chatham, once renowned for a positively gorgeous turnout of its express locomotives, changed to a dark greenish grey, without any relief except a bold sans-serif rendering of the engine number in white paint. The Great Northern painted its goods engines in battleship grey, and the Great Eastern abandoned its rich royal blue for a dull slate grey. These were signs of the times, and some of the old liveries were gone never to re-appear. Then came the grouping of all the old independent railways of Great Britain into four large companies. Only a few of the joint lines and most of the narrow gauge lay outside this tremendous series of mergers.

From 1923 onwards the kaleidoscope of locomotive liveries that had so distinguished the railways of this country was suddenly contracted to four styles, of which three were green – those of the Great Western, of the Southern, and of the London and North Eastern. The London Midland and Scottish Railway retained 'Derby-red', but very soon all, except the top-line passenger types, were painted black. The Somerset and Dorset Joint and the Midland and Great Northern Joint retained their distinctive colours, and there were some gay interludes, as when Sir Nigel Gresley built the Silver Jubilee train in silver throughout, engine and coaches alike – and when the Coronation trains of 1937 were finished in blue. Otherwise it was a case of the traditional Great Western green; Derby-red; and L.N.E.R. apple green. O. V. S. Bulleid, in search for distinction, changed the Southern dark green to a startling synthetic hue known as 'Malachite Green', which is still to be seen on Southern Region passenger coaching stock today.

The nineteen-thirties were a time of great financial anxiety for the railways of Great Britain, and with traffic dwindling many devices of the showman's art were tried to win business. The streamlining of loco-motives had a value far greater to the publicists than to the engineers. At the same time speeds were soaring. For the first time a British train had made a considerably long run at an average speed of more than 80 m.p.h. from start to stop. The maximum speed record went up from 100 m.p.h., or slightly over, made by the Great Western *City of Truro* in 1904, to 108 m.p.h. by the Gresley non-streamlined Pacific *Papyrus* in 1935; to $112\frac{1}{2}$ m.p.h. by the first L.N.E.R. streamliner *Silver Link* later that same year, and then to 114 m.p.h. by the Stanier Pacific

Coronation in 1937. Finally, in 1938, there came the record that is likely to stand for all time – the British and World record for steam, of 126 m.p.h. by the Gresley streamliner *Mallard*.

The Second World War brought an immediate end to all this activity, and the coloured section of this book records the locomotives built for war service, like the austerity 2-8-0, the L.N.E.R. 'B1', and the L.M.S. '8F' 2-8-0, which was ordered to be built for general service by a number of the once-independent railway works. The war was hardly over when nationalization of the railways took place, and the experience of the four main line companies was pooled in the work of a newly formed Railway Executive. From the plethora of strongly individual practices a single set of locomotive designs for the whole country was evolved and, although naturally there were some compromises and mistakes, the British Railways standard locomotives formed a worthy climax to the story. The last design of all, the big '9F' 2-10-0 freight engine, was in every way a remarkable machine.

This picture gallery, extending from the *Locomotion* of 1825 to the *Evening Star* of 1960, forms a deeply impressive record of a great national achievement. The book concerns only locomotives built for service on the home railways. There has been no space to illustrate any of the thousands of locomotives built in Great Britain for service in nearly every corner of the world, which, by opening up the countries, acted as influences for development of trade, industry and education, as well as being incomparable ambassadors of the skill of British engineering workmanship. The era of steam traction on British Railways is now nearly finished. It will go down in history as a period of the greatest social and industrial evolution the world has yet known.

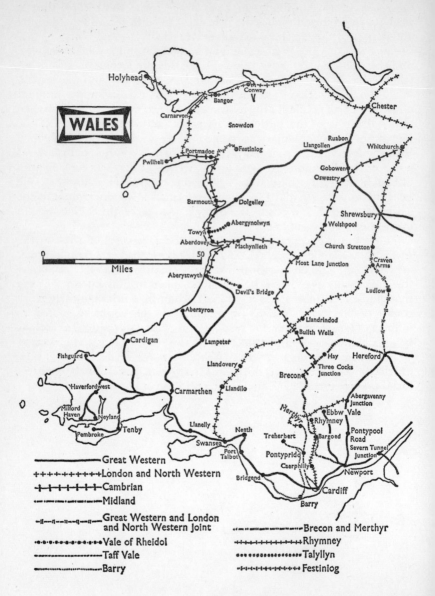

WALES

Holyhead

Conway

Bangor

Carnarvon

Snowdon

Ruabon

Festiniog

Llangollen

Whitchurch

Chester

Portmadoc

Gobowen

Oswestry

Pwllheli

Shrewsbury

Barmouth

Dolgelley

Abergynolwyn

Welshpool

Towyn

Aberdovey

Machynlleth

Church Stretton

Craven Arms

Moat Lane Junction

Ludlow

Aberystwyth

Devil's Bridge

Aberayron

Llandrindod

Builth Wells

Cardigan

Lampeter

Hay

Hereford

Fishguard

Llandovery

Three Cocks Junction

Haverfordwest

Carmarthen

Llandilo

Brecon

Abergavenny Junction

Milford Haven

Neyland

Tenby

Llanelly

Neath

Merthyr

Ebbw Vale

Rhymney

Pembroke

Llandilo

Pontypool Road

Treherbert

Bargoed

Severn Tunnel Junction

Swansea

Port Talbot

Pontypridd

Caerphilly

Newport

Bridgend

Cardiff

Barry

0   50
Miles

——————— Great Western
++++++++++ London and North Western
+|+|+|+|+| Cambrian
·—·—·—·—· Midland
—‖—‖—‖—‖— Great Western and London and North Western Joint
·•·•·•·•·•· Vale of Rheidol
·—·—·—·—· Taff Vale
·············· Barry
·—··—··—·· Brecon and Merthyr
+|+|+|+|+|+ Rhymney
·•·•·•·•·•· Talyllyn
·|·|·|·|·|·|· Festiniog

14

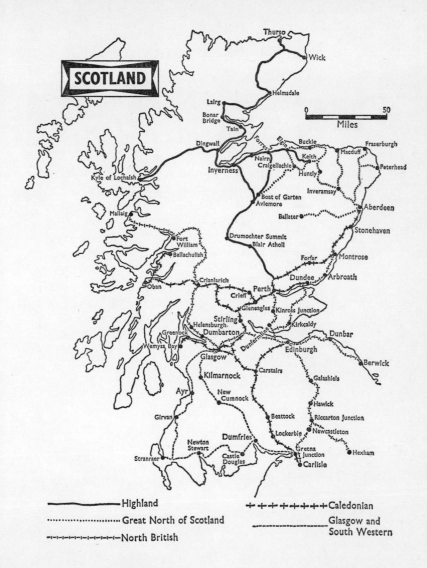

SCOTLAND

Thurso
Wick
Helmsdale
Lairg
Bonar Bridge
Tain
Dingwall
Forres
Elgin
Buckle
Macduff
Fraserburgh
Nairn
Keith
Craigellachie
Peterhead
Inverness
Huntly
Inveramsay
Boat of Garten
Aviemore
Aberdeen
Ballater
Kyle of Lochalsh
Stonehaven
Mallaig
Drumochter Summit
Blair Atholl
Fort William
Ballachulish
Forfar
Montrose
Crianlarich
Dundee
Arbroath
Oban
Crieff
Perth
Gleneagles
Kinross Junction
Stirling
Helensburgh.
Kirkcaldy
Greenock
Dumbarton
Dunbar
Wemyss Bay
Dunfermline
Edinburgh
Glasgow
Berwick
Kilmarnock
Carstairs
Galashiels
Ayr
New Cumnock
Hawick
Girvan
Beattock
Riccarton Junction
Newcastleton
Dumfries
Lockerbie
Newton Stewart
Gretna Junction
Hexham
Stranraer
Castle Douglas
Carlisle

0   50
Miles

——————— Highland   +++++++ Caledonian
·················· Great North of Scotland   Glasgow and
-·-·-·-·-·-·- North British   ————— South Western

15

THE COLOUR ILLUSTRATIONS

A full description of each
locomotive appears between
pages 113 – 186

1 **"Locomotion"**; engine No. 1 of the Stockton and Darlington Railway, built 1825 by George Stephenson.

2 **The "Rocket"**, built by Robert Stephenson 1829, and winner of the Rainhill trials. Liverpool and Manchester Railway.

3 **Planet Type 2–2–0** engine of 1830, inside cylinders;
Liverpool and Manchester Railway.

4 **The "Derwent"**; an 1839 development of Timothy
Hackworth's coal engine for the Stockton and
Darlington Railway.

5 **Edward Bury's 2–2–0**, passenger engine for the London and Birmingham Railway, 1837.

6 **The "North Star"**; Robert Stephenson's 2–2–2 of 1837, for the broad gauge Great Western Railway (7ft).

7 **Crampton Type Engine "London"**; built by
Tulk and Ley, in 1847, for the London and Birmingham Railway.

8 **Allan's "Crewe" Goods**; a 2–4–0 of 1845 built at
Crewe for the Grand Junction Railway.

9   **Sharp 2-2-2**, passenger engine of 1842 for the
South Eastern Railway.

10   **"Firefly" class 2-2-2**, designed by Daniel Gooch
for the Great Western Railway, 1840.

11 **Stephenson Long-Boilered** 4-2-0, of 1847, for
the Southern Division of the London and North
Western Railway.

12 **The "Jenny Lind"**; David Joy's famous 2-2-2
built in 1847 by E. B. Wilson and Co. for the
Brighton railway.

13 **Gooch's Broad Gauge 8-Footer**; first introduced 1847 on the Great Western Railway, here shown final form 1890.

14 **Joseph Beattie's 2-4-0**, express locomotive for the London and South Western Railway, *Herod*. Built 1859.

15 **Stephenson's Long-Boilered Goods**; standard
coal engine of the Stockton and Darlington section
of the North Eastern Railway. One of the latest
examples built 1874.

16 **A Furness Railway "Coppernob"**; a Bury type
0–4–0. An example of 1858, built by Fairbairn and
Co.

17 **Hawthorn Type 2–2–2**; an 1852 express locomotive of the Great Northern Railway.

18 **The Cudworth "Mail" Engine**; crack South Eastern Railway 2–2–2 of 1862.

19 **Craven** 2-2-2, built 1862 for the Brighton railway, shown here as modified by Stroudley.

20 **A Broad Gauge Prodigy**; James Pearson's 9ft 4-2-4 tank engine of 1853, Bristol and Exeter Railway.

21 **A McConnell "Bloomer"**; one of the very celebrated 2–2–2 express locomotives of the L.&N.W.R.
Southern Division.

22 **Highland Railway 2–2–2**; A Scottish variant of
Allan's "Crewe" type, built 1863, here shown as
running in 1874.

23 **Lady of the Lake**; John Ramsbottom's 2–2–2 of
1859 for the Northern Division of the L.&N.W.R.

24 **Sturrock 0–6–0 with Steam Tender**; a heavy
mineral engine of 1863 for the Great Northern
Railway.

25 **Conner 8ft Single**; an express locomotive of 1859
for the Caledonian Railway.

26 **Great North of Scotland Railway**; one of the
earliest British 4-4-0s, designed by W. Cowan, 1865.

27　**Kirtley's "800" Class**; an outstanding 2–4–0 design of 1870 for the Midland Railway.

28　**Robert Sinclair's 2–2–2**; a picturesque and very successful passenger engine of 1862 for the Great Eastern Railway.

29 **A Stirling 8-Footer**; one of the most famous of all
19th Century locomotives, first introduced 1870
on the Great Northern Railway.

30 **A Stroudley "G" Class 2-2-2**; *Petworth*, a design
of 1880 for the London Brighton and South Coast
Railway.

31 **The Tay Bridge Engine**; designed in 1871 for the North British Railway by T. Wheatley this engine went into the river with the collapse of the first Tay Bridge in 1879.

32 **North Eastern Railway "901" Class**; designed by Edward Fletcher, 1872, for the Anglo-Scottish expresses.

33 **David Jones's "F" Class**; a 4–4–0 of 1874 for the
Highland Railway.

34 **London Chatham and Dover Railway**; one of
Martley's "Europa" class 2–4–0s of 1873 used on
the Dover Mails.

35 **North London Railway**; an inside cylinder 4–4–0
tank engine of 1865, in original colours.

36 **A "Small Scotchman"**; a London Chatham and
Dover 0–4–2 tank engine of 1866, one of a class
distinguished by well-known Scottish names.

37 **The Steam Inner Circle**; one of the long-lived
Metropolitan 4–4–0 tanks, originally built in 1864,
here shown as running in 1948

38 **Great Western Railway**; 2–4–0 tank for the
Underground lines in London, and known as the
"Metropolitans".

39　**Dean's Standard Gauge 2–2–2**; a fine express
locomotive of 1878 for the Great Western, here
shown as running in about 1900.

40　**Webb's "Precedent" Class 2–4–0**; London and
North Western Railway: introduced 1874 and 155
built at Crewe Works. *Snowdon* was the last to
remain in traffic, withdrawn 1932.

41 **Glasgow and South Western Railway**; James
Stirling's 4-4-0 of 1873.

42 **Dugald Drummond's N.B.R. 4-4-0** of 1876;
designed specially to work the Waverley route
between Edinburgh and Carlisle.

43 **A Caley "Jumbo"**; Drummond 0–6–0 of 1884 for
the Caledonian Railway.

44 **Webb's Standard Coal Engine**; a London and
North Western design of 1873, of which 500 were
built.

45 **The Dean "Goods"**; the very celebrated G.W.R.
0–6–0 of 1883 in its original livery.

46 **A "Skye Bogie"**; Highland Railway small-wheeled
4–4–0 of 1882 for the Dingwall and Skye line.

47 **Midland Railway**; A Johnson 2–4–0 of 1880 in the
original green livery.

48 **The "Gladstone"**; the celebrated London Brighton
and South Coast 0–4–2 of 1882, designed by W.
Stroudley.

49 **Charles Sacre's 2-2-2**; for the Manchester, Sheffield and Lincolnshire Railway; a distinctive North Country design of 1883.

50 **South Eastern Railway "F" Class**; one of James Stirling's numerous standard 4-4-0s, first introduced 1883.

51 **Metropolitan District Railway**; a Beyer Peacock 4-4-0 tank of 1871, built to the Metropolitan Railway design.

52 **London Tilbury and Southend Railway**; an Adams 4-4-2 tank engine of 1882, as later modified by Thomas Whitelegg.

53 **North London Railway**; an Adams 4–4–0 tank of 1868, as modernised, and running in the 20th Century.

54 **Maryport and Carlisle Railway**; a 2–4–0 passenger engine of 1867, running until 1921.

55 **Matthew Holmes's** 4-4-0, of 1890 for the North
British Railway, ran in the Race to the North in
1895.

56 **Great Eastern Railway**; James Holden's 7ft
2-2-2 of 1888.

57 **Lancashire and Yorkshire Railway**; an Aspinall
4–4–0 of 1891.

58 **W. Adams's Jubilee Class**; a London and South
Western 0–4–2 of 1887.

59 **Worsdell-Von Borries "J" Class**; North Eastern
2-cylinder compound 4–2–2 of 1889.

60 **Midland Railway**; a Johnson 4–4–0 of the "2183"
class, of 1892.

61 **The "Adriatic"**; a London and North Western
Webb 3-cylinder compound of 1889.

62 **Caledonian Railway**; one of the fast and efficient
Drummond 4–4–0s of 1884.

63 **A Dean 7ft 8in 4–2–2**; a classic Great Western
design of 1892, of which 80 were built.

64 **Glasgow and South Western Railway**; one of
James Manson's 4–4–0s of 1892.

65 **A North Eastern "Rail Crusher"**; nicknamed thus because of their great weight, these 4-4-0s of 1892 were designed by Wilson Worsdell.

66 **A Johnson "Spinner"**; a Midland 4-2-2 express locomotive of the 1886–97 period.

67 **London and South Western Railway**; an Adams
outside-cylindered 4-4-0 of 1892.

68 **A Dunalastair 4-4-0**; of the Caledonian Railway,
designed by McIntosh in 1896, this class was one of
the most powerful of 19th Century locomotives.

69 **A Highland "Loch"**; one of David Jones's 4–4–0s
for the Perth – Inverness run. Built 1896.

70 **Great North of Scotland Railway**; engines of
this handsome design were first introduced in 1899.

71 **Webb 4-Cylinder Compound**; one of the longest-
lived of all L.&N.W.R. compound designs. Of this
0–8–0 of 1901 a total of 170 was built.

72 **The First British "Atlantic"**; H. A. Ivatt's "990"
class for the Great Northern, built 1898.

73 **The First British 4–6–0**; the "Jones Goods" of the
Highland Railway introduced in 1894.

74 **The Aspinall Atlantic**; built 1899 for the Lancashire and Yorkshire Railway.

75 **Taff Vale Railway**; one of T. Hurry Riches'
0–6–2 tank engines of 1895.

76 **Barry Railway**; a handsome 0-4-4 passenger
tank engine of 1892.

77 **Rhymney Railway**; a mixed traffic 0–6–2 tank engine of 1909.

78 **Brecon and Merthyr Railway**; a mineral tank engine of 1909.

79 **London Brighton and South Coast Railway**:
R. J. Billinton's "B4" class 4–4–0 of 1899.

80 **An Oil-Fired 4-2-2**, of 1898; James Holden's
locomotives for the Great Eastern Railway Cromer
expresses.

81 **Great Central Railway**; a Pollitt 4–4–0 of 1894 as
modified and superheated by J. G. Robinson.

82 **North Eastern Railway**; one of the celebrated
"R" class 4–4–0s of 1899, some of which were
in service for more than 50 years.

83 **Furness Railway**: a Pettigrew 4-4-0 express passenger engine of 1901.

84 **Cambrian Railways**; a passenger 4-4-0 of 1893 design.

85 **Somerset and Dorset Joint Railway**; a 4–4–0 of
1903 built at the Midland Railway works at Derby.

86 **Midland and Great Northern Joint Railway**;
an express passenger 4–4–0 of 1908, as rebuilt at
Melton Constable from a Midland design of 1894.

87 **Lynton and Barnstaple** narrow gauge railway;
one of the quaint little 2-6-2 tank engines of 1898.

88 **Leek and Manifold Light Railway**; one of the
handsome 2-6-4 tank engines of 1904.

89 **Festiniog Railway**; one of the famous "double-engines", on Robert Fairlie's patent, as running today, but first introduced in 1869.

90 **Snowdon Mountain Railway**; one of the Swiss-built rack locomotives of 1895.

91 **The "Claud Hamilton"**; epoch-marking Great Eastern 4-4-0 of 1900, forerunner of more than 100 of this design.

92 **A Johnson "Belpaire" 4-4-0**, of the Midland Railway, as originally built in 1901 with large bogie tender.

93 **Hull and Barnsley Railway**; one of Matthew
Stirling's express passenger 4-4-0s of 1910.

94 **The "City of Truro"**; the Great Western record
breaker built 1903, attained 100 m.p.h. with an
Ocean Mail special in 1904.

95 **A "Precursor" Class 4-4-0**, of the London and
North Western Railway, No. 1111 *Cerberus*, first
introduced in 1904; eventually the class was 130
strong.

96 **Earle Marsh's "I3" Tank**; a very efficient 4-4-2
of 1908 for the London Brighton and South Coast
Railway.

97 **The De Glehn 4 4 2 "La France"**: French-built compound Atlantic for the Great Western Railway, 1903.

98 **Dugald Drummond's "T9" 4 4 0**: this London and South Western Class of 1899, of which there were 66, were nicknamed the "Greyhounds"

99 **Lancashire and Yorkshire Railways**; one of the
numerous 2-4-2 side tank engines of 1889–1911.

100 **London and South Western Railway**; the "M7"
0-4-4 passenger tank engine of 1897.

101 **Stroudley's "D" Class 0–4–2 Tank**; originally
built in 1873, here shown in the Marsh livery.

102 **Great Eastern Railway**; the 0–6–0 London suburban tank engine of 1890–1902.

103 **"Cardean" of the Caledonian**; one of the most famous of all Scottish locomotives, built 1906.

104 **Glasgow and South Western Railway**; a Manson 4–6–0 of 1903 for the Midland "Pullman" trains.

105 **The Highland "Castle" Class**; a splendid design of 1900, prepared originally by David Jones and completed by Peter Drummond.

106 **A Reid "Atlantic"**; built 1906, later superheated, the premier class of the North British Railway.

107 **A Great Northern "Atlantic"**; first introduced in
1902 by H. A. Ivatt, these engines were the mainstay
of the Anglo-Scottish service south of York for 20
years.

108 **South Eastern and Chatham Railway**; Wainwright's "E" class 4–4–0 of 1905.

109 **A Great Western "Saint"**; outcome of a classic
locomotive development by G. J. Churchward,
begun in 1902.

110 **A Midland Deeley Compound**; developed from
the Smith-Johnson engines of 1902 the superheated
compound of 1913 represented the last word in
Midland locomotive practice.

111 **A "Jersey Lily" of the G.C.R.**; Robinson's handsome Atlantic design of 1904.

112 **The "Great Bear"**; Churchward's experimental Pacific of 1908, Great Western Railway.

113 **A Brighton "Atlantic"**; Earle-Marsh's 4–4–2 locomotive of 1905 for the seaside expresses of the L.B.&S.C.R.

114 **North Staffordshire Railway**; John H. Adams's 4–4–2 superheated tank engine of 1911.

115 **The "Abergavenny"**; Earle-Marsh's 4–6–2 tank
engine of 1910, for the Brighton line.

116 **The "Immingham" Class 4–6–0**; Robinson's
express goods engine of 1907 for the Great Central
Railway.

117 **London Tilbury and Southend Railway**;
Thomas Whitelegg's 4–4–2 express tank engine of
1907–9.

118 **The Class "X" Hump Shunters**; of the North
Eastern Railway, built 1909 for work in marshalling
yards.

119 **The "Coronation" Engine of 1911**; one of the very celebrated "George the Fifth" class 4-4-0s of the London and North Western Railway.

120 **A Great Central "Director"**: J. G. Robinson's express passenger 4-4-0 of 1913.

121 **Midland Railway**; Fowler's Class 2 superheated
4-4-0 of 1913.

122 **Dugald Drummond's "D15"**; introduced 1912
on the L.&S.W.R. these handsome 4-4-0s were his
last locomotive design.

123 **Great Eastern Railway**; the "1500" class 4–6–0
of 1912 (later known as L.N.E.R. "B12").

124 **A North Eastern "Z"**; one of Sir Vincent Raven's
3-cylinder Atlantics of 1911.

125 **A "Prince of Wales" 4-6-0**; a very successful
London and North Western design of 1911; engine
No. 1537 *Enchantress*.

126 **A Drummond 4-Cylinder 4-6-0**; one of the
"T14" class of 1911 (L.&S.W.R.) nicknamed the
"Paddleboats".

127 **A North Western "Claughton"**; Bowen-Cooke's
4-cylinder 4–6–0 first built at Crewe in 1913, engine
No. 668 *Rupert Guinness*.

128 **L. Billinton's Giant 4 6 4**; the *Charles C. Macrae*
of 1914 for the Brighton expresses.

129 **A Great Northern "Mogul"**; Gresley's "K2"
class 2–6–0 of 1914.

130 **A "River" Class 4–6–0**; originally built for the
Highland in 1915, but transferred to the Caledonian
and here shown in the C.R. livery.

131   **Churchward's Masterpiece**; the Great Western
4-cylinder 4-6-0 "Star" class, introduced 1907, and
superheated from 1909 onwards.

132   **A Pickersgill 4-4-0**; for the Caledonian Railway,
introduced 1916, of a class eventually numbering 48.

133 **Glasgow and South Western Railway**; Peter
Drummond's express goods 2-6-0 of 1915.

134 **A North British "Glen"**; a very powerful 4-4-0
of 1913 designed by W. P. Reid for the West
Highland line.

135 **Somerset and Dorset Joint Railway**; one of the special 2–8–0 freight engines designed and built at Derby in 1914.

136 **Caledonian Railway**; a Pickersgill outside cylindered 4–6–0 of 1916.

137 **A "Super D" o–8–o Goods**, of the London and
North Western Railway, introduced 1912; class
eventually 295 strong.

138 **North Staffordshire Railway**; Hookham's 0–6–4
passenger tank engine of 1916.

139 **A North Eastern "T2"**; a heavy mineral 0–8–0 of
1913.

140 **A Highland Railway "Clan"**; a 4–6–0 of 1919
designed by Christopher Cumming.

141 **The Gresley "K3" 2–6–0**; originally built for the Great Northern, in 1920. The class became an L.N.E.R. standard.

142 **South Eastern and Chatham Railway**; Maunsell's "N" class mixed traffic 2–6–0 of 1917.

143 **A Maunsell "E1"** 4–4–0; rebuilt from class E in
1919 for the S.E.&C.R. Continental Boat trains.

144 **Furness Railway**; E. Sharples's 4–6–4 tank engine
of 1920 for heavy intermediate duty.

145 **The Lickey Bank Engine**; Midland Railway
4-cylinder 0–10–0 (Big Bertha).

146 **The "N2" Suburban Tank of 1921**; designed by
H. N. Gresley for the Great Northern local services.

147 **Great Northern Railway**; Gresley's 3-cylinder
2–8–0 mineral engine of 1921.

148 **R. Whitelegg's Baltic Tank**; of 1922, for the Glasgow and South Western Clyde coast services.

149 **Metropolitan Railway**; Charles Jones's 4–4–4 express tank engine of 1920 for outer residential services.

150 **J. G. Robinson's Historic 2–8–0**; designed in 1911 for the Great Central Railway; adopted as a War Office standard, in 1914-18, and built to a total of 521 for army services overseas.

151 **A Great Western "Castle"**; a later example, the
Isambard Kingdom Brunel, of the famous design
introduced in 1923 by C. B. Collett.

152 **Lancashire and Yorkshire Railway**; a "Class
8" 4-cylinder 4–6–0 of 1920.

153 **The First Gresley Pacific**; No. 1470 *Great Northern* of the G.N.R. built 1922.

154 **Sir Vincent Raven's Pacific**; the climax of North Eastern locomotive design, built in 1922.

155 **The "King Arthur" Class**; Southern Railway express passenger 4–6–0 of 1925.

156 **An L.M.S. Standard Compound**; built from 1923 onwards as a result of the successful trials of the standard Midland type 4–4–0.

157 **An L.M.S. Standard Goods**; the "4F" 0–6–0,
developed from Fowler's Midland design.

158 **The "Sandringham" Class 4–6–0**; built 1928,
for the East Anglian services of the London and
North Eastern Railway.

159 **The "Lord Nelson"**; Maunsell's 4-cylinder 4–6–0
for the Southern Railway, built 1926.

160 **The "Royal Scot" Class 4–6–0**; an L.M.S.R.
standard design of 1927 that became world famous.

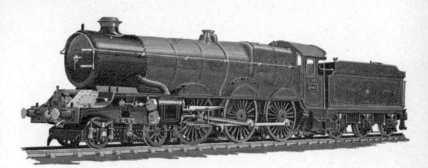

161　**The "King George V"**; the ultimate development
on the G.W.R. of the Churchward 4-cylinder 4–6–0
design, built at Swindon 1927.

162　**The Gresley Super-Pacific**; a very famous
engine, *Papyrus*, of the L.N.E.R. "A3" class.

163 **An L.M.S. Horwich Mogul**; the 2–6–0 mixed traffic design of 1926.

164 **The G.W.R. "Hall" Class**; a smaller wheeled variant (1924) of the Churchward "Saint" class.

165 **Gresley's "Shire" Class 4–4–0**; a 3-cylinder
4–4–0 of 1927 for general passenger service.

166 **A Beyer-Garratt 2–6–0 † 0–6–2**; freight engine
for the L.M.S.R. introduced 1927.

167 **L.M.S. "5XP" (Baby Scot)**; of 1930, later known officially as the "Patriot" class.

168 **A Southern "School"**; the most powerful 4-4-0s in Europe, introduced by R. E. L. Maunsell in 1929.

169 **A Pannier Tank 0–6–0** of the Great Western
Railway. Introduced in 1929 this class eventually
consisted of 790 engines.

170 **A Stanier "Black Five"**; a standard L.M.S. mixed
traffic 4–6–0 of 1934 design.

171   **A Gresley "P2" 2-8-2**, for the L.N.E.R., one of a class of 6, representing the only 8-coupled express locomotives to run in Britain; introduced 1934.

172   **A World Record Breaker**; Gresley's streamlined Pacific *Mallard*, which attained 126 m.p.h. in 1938.

173 **The "Princess Elizabeth"**; one of Stanier's "Princess Royal" class Pacifics of 1933 for the L.M.S.R.

174 **The "Coronation" of 1937**; the L.M.S. streamlined Pacific design for the Coronation Scot service.

175 **A "Green Arrow" 2-6-2**; Gresley's very successful mixed traffic design for the London and North Eastern Railway.

176 **A Stanier "8F" 2-8-0**; originally designed for the L.M.S.R. but adopted as a national standard engine in World War II.

177 **An L.M.S. "Jubilee" 4-6-0**; introduced 1934 by
Sir William Stanier, for general express service.

178 **"Sir William A. Stanier F.R.S."**; a Pacific of
1947 representing the final development of the
L.M.S. Stanier Pacifics.

179 **The Vale of Rheidol Line**; the only narrow gauge section of British Railways, a Swindon built 2–6–2 tank engine of 1923.

180 **Talyllyn Railway**; the original engine of the railway, built 1865, as running today under the auspices of the Talyllyn Railway Preservation Society.

181 **Isle of Man Railway**; A Beyer-Peacock 2–4–0
tank engine of 1873, in the livery of today.

182 **Romney, Hythe and Dymchurch Railway**; a
15-inch gauge 4–8–2 express locomotive *Hercules*.

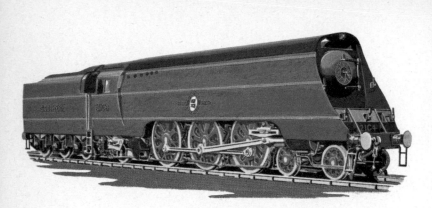

183 **"Merchant Navy" Class**; Pacific designed by
O. V. S. Bulleid, in 1941, as originally built with air
smoothed casing.

184 **A Thompson "B1"** 4–6–0; introduced by L.N.E.R.
in 1942 for general utility service.

185 **The Rebuilt "Royal Scot"** of 1943, including many new features and the Stanier taper boiler.

186 **Austerity 2–8–0 of 1942**; built for wartime service at home and overseas to designs of R. A. Riddles.

187 **The Peppercorn "A1"**; the L.N.E.R. Pacific of
1947, here shown in British Railways colours.

188 **A "Britannia" Pacific**; a British Railways standard design of 1951, the *Hereward the Wake*.

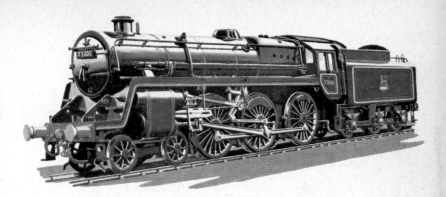

189　**A "BR5" Mixed Traffic 4–6–0**; a general utility engine developed from the Stanier "Black Five".

190　**A "West Country" 4–6–2**; formerly of the Bulleid air-smoothed design, but here seen rebuilt with conventional valve gear, and outer casing removed.

191 **A "BR4" Standard 2-6-0**; designed by R. A.
Riddles for light general utility services.

192 **The "Evening Star"**; last steam locomotive built
for service in Great Britain; one of the Riddles
"9F" 2-10-0s.

1 **'Locomotion';** engine No. 1 of the Stockton and Darlington Railway.

This celebrated engine, built in September 1825, was the first steam locomotive to be used on a public railway. It was a development of the type George Stephenson had worked up on the Killingworth Colliery lines, and included a number of features that were fairly common among the primitive, pioneer steam locomotives of what may be termed the pre-*Rocket* age. This engine is now preserved, and displayed on a pedestal in Darlington station. A point that immediately strikes the onlooker is the construction of the wheels – built up from a number of iron castings dowelled together. The valve gear was on the top of the boiler, and the two cylinders were mounted with their axes vertically, and the lower parts of each cylinder *inside the boiler*. There was one single flue 2 ft. in diameter, and at the front end this flue was bent round and continued upward as a chimney. The boiler pressure was 50 lb. per sq. in. When the engine was first put into service it would not steam, and the single flue had to be replaced by a return flue. The little tender was made entirely of wood, carrying a sheet-iron tank for water. This engine ran during the public opening of the railway, on September 27, 1825, and though it was far from successful in its original form its work was such as to provide encouragement and promise to all those who had faith in the establishment of a railway system operated by steam locomotives.

2 **The 'Rocket';** Liverpool and Manchester Railway.

While very far from being the father of all steam locomotives the *Rocket*, winner of the ever-famous Rainhill trials of 1829, could certainly lay claim to be the very first one to be reasonably successful and reliable in service. In the Science Museum at South Kensington there are, virtually, two *Rockets*. One, an old and obviously well-used machine, is the original engine, though very much altered from the condition in which she won the Rainhill prize for George and Robert Stephenson. The second is an exact replica of the original, in her Rainhill condition, in the gay livery she sported for the trials. The *Rocket* as originally built, and as illustrated here, had her cylinders mounted at a steeply inclined angle high up on the side of the boiler. This gave her an awkward swaying action at speed, and some little time after she went into regular service on the Liverpool and Manchester Railway the position of the cylinders was changed. The other outstanding feature of the original *Rocket* was the use of the multitubular boiler, and the passing of the exhaust steam from the cylinders through a narrowing passage to an orifice in the smokebox. The blastpipe, for so it became known, produced a draught through the boiler tubes and assisted in accelerating combustion of the fuel, and the rapid raising of steam.

3 **Planet Type 2-2-0;** Liverpool and Manchester Railway.

One of the most marked characteristics in the working of the *Rocket*, observed very clearly during the Rainhill trials, and criticized by opponents of the Stephensons, was the swaying jerky action of the engine, attributable to the mounting of the cylinders high up on the side of the smokebox. Later engines of the 'Rocket' type had the cylinders mounted more nearly horizontal, but still outside the frames. The use of inside cylinders on the *Planet* in 1830 – probably the very first case in the world – was not wholly due to a desire to get smoother riding, but due to a suggestion made to Robert Stephenson by Richard Trevithick the great Cornish pioneer, who had found in repairing an old beam engine that he obtained an almost sensational economy of fuel by fitting a jacket round the cylinder to prevent loss of heat by radiation. On the *Planet* Stephenson enclosed the cylinders within the smokebox. The engine also incorporated the first use of 'sandwich' frames, which were formed of ash or oak, strengthened by iron plates inside and out. These gave flexibility and a great strength, and were a distinctive feature – for example – of many broad gauge locomotives on the Great Western Railway in later years. The *Planet* was thus very much a landmark in locomotive history.

4 The 'Derwent'; Stockton and Darlington Railway.

Hackworth had been associated with the Stephensons, father and son, from the very inception of the Stockton and Darlington Railway; but after its opening to the public circumstances arose to leave him very much on his own, and he was faced with the poor steaming qualities of the *Locomotion* and other engines working on the line. It was Hackworth who conceived the idea of putting a return bend in the flue, running it the length of the boiler twice, and so lengthening the time that the hot gases of combustion were in proximity to the water. After some experiments this idea was incorporated in a new engine, the *Royal George*, built in 1827, and in so doing Hackworth incorporated what we should now regard as a very quaint idea. The use of the return flue meant that the firebox had to be at the same end of the engine as the chimney. So Hackworth provided two tenders – one propelled in front of the engine carrying the coal and the fireman, and the second at the rear, carrying the water tank, or barrel, and the driver. A beautiful example of this type of engine has been preserved at Darlington, the *Derwent*, which was built by Alfred Kitching and Company, in 1839. Engines of this type were built down to the year 1846, and some were still in regular service on the Stockton and Darlington line in 1875.

5 Edward Bury's 2-2-0; London and Birmingham Railway.

Edward Bury was once described as a man strongly endowed with the commercial instinct. He certainly contrived to play, very successfully, the rôle of Locomotive Superintendent of the London and Birmingham Railway and contractor for the supply of locomotives at one and the same time. His engines were light, ingeniously constructed, and so very cheap; and in his rôle as user of them he saw to it that they were not overworked. The distinguishing feature of all his engines was the use of bar frames, which gave them a light, spidery appearance. They had circular fireboxes, with a steam dome and safety valve on the top. The passenger engines on the London and Birmingham were of the 2-2-0 type, while the goods, otherwise similar, were 0-4-0. If one engine were not enough to do the job he put on two, three, and sometimes even four on one train! It was all good for the locomotive trade. Like many engines of those early days the Bury's rode badly, partly because of the very short wheelbase, and the lightness of the tenders. The London and Birmingham nevertheless remained a home of these light four-wheeled engines long after all other main lines had abandoned them for longer and larger engines, and in view of the heavy traffic on the line, and the multitudes of engines necessary to work it, the four-wheeled Bury's, whether of the 2-2-0 or 0-4-0 type, have a special place in railway history.

6 The 'North Star'; Great Western Railway.

From its inception the Great Western Railway in many respects stood in isolation from the rest of the country, through its adoption of the broad gauge, 7 ft., in contrast to the standard gauge of 4 ft. 8½ in. used on most other railways in Great Britain. Brunel was the architect of the broad gauge, and at first he took direct responsibility for ordering the locomotives. It must be admitted that he saddled the G.W.R. with a poor lot – with one outstanding exception. The *North Star* came to the Great Western almost by accident, as it were. It was built by Robert Stephenson and Co. for service in America on the New Orleans Railway. It was actually shipped, but through business difficulties delivery was not taken, and it was returned to England. On its arrival back it was adapted to run on the 7 ft. gauge and sold to the Great Western. A replica of it is now housed in the G.W.R. Museum at Swindon, and looking on this one can quite appreciate Brunel's comment, that it would make a handsome ornament in the most elegant drawing-room. It was upon the general layout of the *North Star* that Daniel Gooch based the design of his very successful 'Firefly' class of 2-2-2 express locomotives. The original *North Star* was withdrawn from service in 1870, and for many years it was kept at Swindon. It was scrapped in 1906, and the present replica was constructed for the Railway Centenary celebrations in 1925.

7 Crampton Type Engine 'London'; London and Birmingham Railway.

Thomas Russell Crampton was one of the great characters of early railway days. Unlike most of the great pioneers he was born in comparatively genteel circumstances, and it was not until he was 23 years of age that he took his first post as an engineer. From then onwards he proved himself a prolific, if rather fanciful inventor. He will always be remembered by the 'Crampton' type of locomotive, which has a single pair of large-diameter driving wheels at the extreme rear end. The idea was to leave the forward part of the locomotive completely clear of driving axles and running gear so as to use a large boiler. His engines were tried on many railways in Great Britain, but although they were fast runners they were not generally successful. The engine illustrated in our picture was built in 1847 by Tulk and Ley, and had 8 ft. diameter driving wheels. It is credited with runs at over 50 m.p.h. on the London and Birmingham section of the L.N.W.R. main line. On the Continent of Europe Crampton had far greater success, and in France and Germany the type was well liked, and up to the year 1864 no fewer than 300 had been built. In France indeed the phrase 'Prendre le Crampton' was synonymous with 'going by train'! A magnificent example has been preserved, and today is still in full working order. It made some special runs as recently as the summer of 1963.

8 Allan's 'Crewe' Goods; Grand Junction Railway.

At the time of the great amalgamation of 1846, by which the London and Birmingham, the Grand Junction, and the Manchester and Birmingham Railways merged to form the London and North Western, Alexander Allan was 'foreman of locomotives' on the Grand Junction, at Crewe. To overcome difficulties with broken crank axles on the older engines Allan developed a new design using outside cylinders, with the cylinders themselves ensconced in a massive arrangement of double framing. This proved an extremely sound mechanical job, and large numbers of locomotives of both 2-2-2 and 2-4-0 types were built at Crewe for service on the Northern Division of the newly-formed London and North Western Railway. Engines of this type were the first to work over the formidable obstacle of Shap Summit, among the Westmorland Fells. In later years Allan was much in demand as a locomotive consultant, and engines of this same general type were used on various sections of the Caledonian Railway. On the L.N.W.R. all the old Crewe engines, both 2-2-2 passenger and 2-4-0 goods, were named; the nameplates were of the plain brass plate type standard throughout the entire existence of the L.N.W.R., while the great majority of the names allotted to the Allan engines were handed down from one generation of Crewe locomotives to another. Between 1845 and 1858 a total of 396 engines of the Allan type were built at Crewe for service on the L.N.W.R.; 158 were of the 2-2-2 wheel arrangement, and 238 were 2-4-0s.

9 **Sharp 2-2-2;** South Eastern Railway. In contrast to the novel, almost freakish long-boilered express engines favoured by Stephenson's in the 1840s, some of the other locomotive builders concentrated on a simple, straightforward design, when they were left to their own predilections. Sharp, Roberts and Co., later Sharp, Stewart, and eventually a constituent of the North British Locomotive Company, developed a simple 2-2-2 design, with outside frames in which the characteristic feature was the curve of the running plate over the driving wheel axlebox. This was done to avoid leaving excessively-deep horn guides for the leading and trailing coupled wheels. The example illustrated is one of a batch used on the South Eastern Railway from the opening of the line. At that time the main line to Dover went via Redhill, and under a working arrangement with the London and Croydon Railway the locomotive stocks of the two companies were pooled. Nearly all the Sharp 2-2-2s contributed to the pool by the South Eastern Railway were named, and included such quaint Saxon titles as *Eadbald*, *Ethelred* and *Egbert* together with invaders of the Kentish shores like *Hengist* and *Horsa*.

10 **'Firefly' Class 2-2-2;** Great Western Railway.
When Gooch was appointed Locomotive Superintendent of the G.W.R. his chief, the great Isambard Kingdom Brunel had already ordered a number of locomotives. They proved to be a poor lot, and of the original deliveries only the *North Star* from Stephenson's, reference 6, had any degree of reliability. Gooch was authorized to purchase many more engines, and he took the *North Star* design, and incorporated in it many great improvements, particularly in the provision of a much more adequate boiler and firebox. The result was the very famous 'Firefly' class, of which the first examples were put on the road in 1840. They were enormous engines for the period, and striking in appearance not only for their great width, but by the huge bell-mouthed chimney, the boiler lagging of polished timber, and the haycock type of firebox, the top of which was covered in polished copper sheet. No fewer than 62 of these engines were built between 1840 and 1842, and they put the Great Western far in advance of any other company so far as engine power and speed was concerned. One of the finest recorded performances was in 1844 on the opening of the line throughout from London to Exeter. On the return trip, with the engine *Actaeon*, the entire journey was done in 4 hr. 40 min. at an average speed of $41\frac{1}{2}$ m.p.h. over a distance of 194 miles. This was quite outstanding for the year 1844.

11 **Stephenson Long-boilered 4-2-0;** London and North Western Railway.
The long-boilered type of locomotive was used in many applications by Robert Stephenson and Co., and for passenger work the 2-2-2 wheel arrangement was at first adopted. Some were put into service on the York and North Midland Railway, others in East Anglia, and there was the notorious *White Horse of Kent*. All these engines were alike in having the wheels close together in the centre, leaving considerable overhangs at front and rear. And all were dangerously unsteady when they worked up to speed. The *White Horse of Kent* caused the death of several enginemen through derailments and overturning. Then Stephenson tried a different arrangement of the wheels, and the

London and North Western engine illustrated had the driving wheels at the back and two pairs of carrying wheels, spaced wide apart, under the front end of the engine. The middle pair of wheels were flangeless. Some engines of this type running on the L.&N.W.R. had driving wheels of no less than 7 ft. in diameter, the largest ever applied to a Stephenson long-boilered engine. But despite the re-arrangement of the wheels these engines were little better as vehicles than the 2-2-2 type, and their life was relatively short. They stand out as a curiosity, but one nevertheless that was at one time highly favoured by the pioneer firm of locomotive builders in the world.

12 **The 'Jenny Lind';** Brighton Railway.
The designing of this famous and beautiful engine is one of the 'romances' of British railway history. Joy worked for E. B. Wilson and Company, of the Railway Foundry, Leeds, and after he had been sent to Brighton to gather particulars of the new express locomotives required the question was thrown into the melting pot, and Wilson's were told to supply whatever they liked. There was much disagreement among the directors as to what to build, and it was in a feeling of frustration that Joy went home for the weekend. In the quiet of his own home he looked at the problem anew, began to sketch, and by Sunday evening the *Jenny Lind* was designed. Its particular features were the inside framing for the driving wheels, outside frames for the leading and trailing, and what was then quite a large boiler, carrying a pressure of 120 lb. per sq. in. The classical fluted style of the dome, and safety valve column was a feature of all Wilson's products at that time. After the success of the first engines of this type on the Brighton railway, Wilson supplied 'Jennys' to many other railways, and at the height of their popularity the Railway Foundry was building them at the rate of one per week. Some of the most picturesque, so far as outward finish was concerned, were those on the Oxford, Worcester and Wolverhampton Railway, which eventually became part of the Great Western. Others of the same general design were used on the York and North Midland Railway.

13 **Gooch's Broad Gauge 8-footer;** Great Western Railway.
Spurred by the exciting stimulus of the 'Battle of the Gauges', locomotive development on the Great Western Railway was extremely rapid in the eighteen-forties. Brunel had claimed superior travel in every way as the advantage of his 7 ft. gauge, and when its continuance was challenged to the extent of setting up a Royal Commission on Railway Gauges Daniel Gooch built a series of locomotives at Swindon Works that gave a performance far superior to anything then running on the standard 4 ft. 8½ in. gauge. The culmination of this rapid development was the *Iron Duke* of 1847. This remarkable engine was the forerunner of 23 more, built at Swindon in 1847 to 1851, and 7 more were added to the stock in 1854-5. These engines, rebuilt and no more than slightly modernized, lasted for the entire remaining period of the broad gauge, until May 1892, by which time their appearance had been changed to that shown in our picture of *Tornado*. Originally they had no cabs, and the boilers were clothed with varnished wood lagging. A peculiarity of the broad gauge was that none of the locomotives carried numbers. They were recognized only by their names – a fine lot, symbolical of the speed and prowess of the Great Western in broad gauge days: *Amazon, Courier, Rover, Swallow, Lightning, Warlock* and so on.

14 **Joseph Beattie's 2-4-0;** London and South Western Railway.
For many years the London and South

Western locomotive department, at Nine Elms, was ruled with a rod of iron by Joseph Beattie. He was not only a martinet but a lover of gadgets in engineering design, and his engines were fitted with innumerable fancy gadgets for improving their thermal efficiency. The 2-4-0 express locomotives with 6 ft. 6 in. coupled wheels were the nearest approach to a standard class at the period 1860–70. There were 62 of them in all, built between 1859 and 1875, and in that period they did the bulk of the express passenger work between London and Salisbury, and London and Bournemouth. They carried a most ornate and beautiful livery, but some of their names were rather forbidding – strongly suggestive of the hard, fiery-natured designer. Our picture shows *Herod*. Other Beattie engines had such titles as *Firebrand, Tartar, Plutus, Volcano, Vulcan*! Joseph Beattie followed a positive crusade towards coal saving, and his engines had some extraordinary designs of fireboxes, which certainly saved coal, but introduced many points of leakage. The drivers and firemen must have had many trials and tribulations in nursing Beattie's gadgets along. But it would have been more than their lives were worth to complain, or suggest alternatives!

15 **Stephenson's Long-boilered Goods;** North Eastern Railway.
By the end of the 'thirties' of last century many firms had entered the field of locomotive building, and at that early date in railway history the railway companies mostly had insufficient experience to specify their needs precisely. They had to choose between the specialities of different builders, and he who could claim novelty or increased efficiency got the most consideration. Robert Stephenson & Co. came out with the idea of the 'long-boilered' engine, in which all wheels were placed ahead of the firebox, so that there was no restriction on its size. But the firebox was not the only consideration,

and a long boiler needs a very fierce draught to make it steam freely. In main line express service the long-boilered type was a failure, but in heavy mineral service it was remarkably successful. In the latter kind of service one did not have to cater for continuous steaming. A coal train might be held up for half an hour or more, and then the long boiler proved a most useful reservoir for storing up a supply of steam for the next pull-away. On the Stockton and Darlington Railway the 'long-boilered' 0-6-0 was the standard freight engine down to the year 1875, and the engine illustrated, which has been restored to its original condition and preserved in the Railway Museum at York, was in regular service until 1922.

16 **A Furness Railway 'Coppernob'.**
Bury's design of bar-framed four-wheeled engine was adopted by a number of railways in the early days, and one of these was the Furness. Four engines of Bury's own manufacture were purchased in 1844–6, and one of these, No. 3, has fortunately been preserved and is now to be seen in the Transport Museum at Clapham. The engine illustrated is one of a larger type built later by Fairbairn. No. 3 has had a long and fascinating history. After 54 years' service on the Furness Railway it was taken out of traffic and enthroned on a pedestal at Barrow Central Station, surrounded by an enormous canopied glass case. Eventually there came the second world war, and in the sustained enemy attacks on the arms towns Barrow suffered severely and the central station was literally razed to the ground. *Coppernob*'s case escaped a direct hit, but all the glass was blown out, and the precious old relic left perilously exposed. In clearing up the mess, however, *Coppernob* was not forgotten, and she was removed to Horwich Works. For many years she remained safe, but occult from public gaze; but now, restored to her former glory, in the magnificent iron-ore

red of the Furness Railway, she is on show again, though still bearing some of the dents and scars as a memento of that terrible night at Barrow when the old station was destroyed.

17 Hawthorn Type 2-2-2; Great Northern Railway.

Before the locomotive superintendents of the leading railways began to develop a design style of their own one could usually tell the manufacture of any locomotive by the distinctive shapes of the chimneys, domes, safety valve columns and so on. The engine illustrated was one of a class of twelve very fine express locomotives built by R. & W. Hawthorn in 1852–3. On the G.N.R. they were always known as the 'Large Hawthorns', to distinguish them from a batch of 20 of generally similar appearance, but smaller dimensions, supplied in 1850. The 'Large Hawthorns' had 6 ft. 6 in. driving wheels, and what was a very large boiler for that period. They did excellent work on the line, and one of them was concerned in a most spectacular smash at Retford. This was engine No. 210, and on this occasion she was running the northbound Flying Scotsman. By some mischance a goods train of the Manchester, Sheffield and Lincolnshire Railway had been allowed to proceed right across the main line. The driver of No. 210 on sighting the obstruction realized he could not stop in time, so he did the only alternative thing – put on full steam, and charged full tilt into the goods train! He scattered the light wooden trucks like match splinters and took the express safely through.

18 The Cudworth 'Mail' Engine; South Eastern Railway.

The South Eastern Railway began its existence in a most complicated and roundabout way. Seeing that it formed the Royal Mail route to the Continent via Folkestone and Dover, and carried the mails from London to India and the Far East on the first stage of their journey, the original route to Dover, via Redhill, was a very poor one. East of Redhill, however, the line was direct enough, and laid out for fast running, but the working of the mail trains was complicated by the use of the old tidal harbour at Folkestone, which meant that the running of the boat trains had to be fitted in to suit the tides! Despite the difficulties and the handicaps some fine running was done with the 'Tidals', as the Folkestone boat trains were always known, and Cudworth's 2-2-2 express locomotives of 1862 were in the very front rank for their time. Such was their success that they were on the job for the best part of 20 years. The South Eastern had a reputation for sloth and inefficient working in Victorian times; and on the secondary and local services that criticism was justified. No such stigma was attached either to the Continental Mail Expresses that ran to the Admiralty Pier at Dover, or to the Folkestone 'Tidals'. The Cudworth 2-2-2s ran these trains up to the limit of speed permitted on the line, namely 60 m.p.h.

19 Craven 2-2-2; Brighton railway.

No set of illustrations of what might be termed the 'Middle Ages' of the Victorian railway development in Great Britain would be complete without at least one example of the work of John Chester Craven, Locomotive Superintendent of the Brighton Railway. The trouble is, there are so many examples to choose from. Craven's policy was the very opposite of standardization, and he built individual engines for special jobs. It seemed, indeed, that at one time he had a different kind of engine for each of the Brighton Railway's many country branch lines. His main line passenger engines were strong, reliable engines, and the one chosen for illustration was among the last built at Brighton under his superintendence. They were put to work in 1862. Certain features may be noted, especially the shelter for the enginemen, which had no sides. To the travelling public these engines became more familiar in the form illustrated, when they had been modified by Craven's successor William Stroudley, who painted them in his famous yellow livery. The driving wheels were 6 ft. 6 in., and the cylinders 17 in. diameter by 22 in. stroke. The numerous different designs left by Craven did not appeal to Stroudley's ideas of standardization, and though these Craven 2-2-2s were good engines in their way they had relatively short lives, and the two of them were scrapped in 1888 and 1891.

20 A Broad Gauge Prodigy; James Pearson's 9 ft. 4-2-4 tank engine, Bristol and Exeter Railway.

Although the broad gauge main line south-westwards from Bristol had been strongly sponsored by the Great Western, it was at first an independent company, and its management enjoyed displaying its independence on many occasions – sometimes to the considerable embarrassment of the Great Western. James Pearson was locomotive superintendent, and he designed the extraordinary 4-2-4 tank engines, with a single pair of driving wheels 9 ft. in diameter. Eight of them were originally built, and they handled the express traffic between Bristol and Exeter for several years. Our picture shows their peculiar appearance from the rear end, but they were no less extraordinary at the front. The cylinders were partly enclosed in the base of the D-shaped smokebox, but the latter was so short from front to back that part of the cylinders protruded at the front. They had also a most unusual form of suspension of the main driving axles. The housing for the outer helical spring can be seen hanging down outside the driving wheel. The original engines were scrapped after a life of about 16 years, and four new engines with 8 ft. 10 in. driving wheels

were built in their place. After the Bristol and Exeter Railway was absorbed by the Great Western they were converted into 4-2-2 tender engines.

21 A McConnell 'Bloomer'; L. & N. W.R. Southern Division.

For some years after the amalgamation of 1847 the London and North Western Railway was organized in two separate divisions, each with its own locomotive superintendent, and works. The practice of the Southern Division, at Wolverton, under J. E. McConnell, was the very opposite of that of Trevithick and Allan, at Crewe. The latter used the very smallest engines that would do the job, whereas McConnell 'built big', and put machines on the road that were generally ahead of their time. Technically his various 2-2-2 express locomotives were characterized by large boilers, and great freedom in running; but externally they created interest by having all the bearings inside. It was a time when Mrs Amelia Bloomer was advocating certain rather startling changes in female attire that shocked Victorian society, and McConnell's new engines, with all their wheels exposed, were immediately nicknamed the 'Bloomers'. There were three varieties: the original 'large' class of 1851, which is illustrated; a smaller variety, introduced in 1854, and three engines of 1861, which were known as the 'Extra Large Bloomers'. No less striking was the livery of the Southern Division – in its vivid scarlet. One has only to compare the Crampton engine London and one of the Bloomers, with the Allan 2-4-0 and the Lady of the Lake to appreciate the astonishing contrast between the contemporary styles of Wolverton and Crewe Works.

22 Highland Railway 2-2-2.

The success of the Allan Crewe-type locomotives, in their mechanical soundness and simplicity, tended to lead to the perpetuation of the design beyond the point where it was really suitable. Of this there was no more striking case than that of the Highland Railway. Allan was consultant to the Inverness and Nairn Railway; but while his little 2-2-2s were ideal for the level run along the shores of the Moray Firth they were certainly *not* suitable for the line across the Grampians which attained an altitude of 1484 ft. above sea level in the Pass of Drumochter. Nevertheless no fewer than 54 locomotives of the Allan 6-wheeled type – 24 of the 2-2-2 type, and 30 of the 2-4-0 – were supplied to the Highland Railway between 1855 and 1871. At first they were supplied virtually identical in appearance to the Crewe engines, with their rather gaunt outline. But they were rendered much neater and prettier in appearance in Stroudley's day, and painted in the famous 'yellow' livery that he took to the Brighton Railway. Our picture shows engine No. 32 of the Highland, originally supplied in October 1863, but as running from 1874 onwards. She was originally named *Sutherland,* but took the name *Cluny* in 1874, exchanging names with No. 55, which was converted from a 2-2-2 to a 2-4-0 at that time. As shown, *Cluny* has the David Jones livery, and chimney with louvres. The cab dates from Stroudley's time. Originally these engines, like their counterparts on the L.N.W.R., had no cabs.

23 **Lady of the Lake;** Northern Division of the L.&N.W.R.

These dainty little engines, designed by John Ramsbottom, and built, to a total of 60, at Crewe between 1859 and 1865, were originally intended for the Irish Mail traffic between London and Holyhead. Ramsbottom was not a believer in large engines, and throughout the years of his chieftainship at Crewe he built machines that were about the smallest and lightest that would do the work. The 'Ladies' were ideal for the job when they were first introduced, and although they

had a peculiar lateral wobble when running at speed they were popular with their crews, and did good work. They were the first locomotives in the world to be equipped with apparatus for picking up water at speed, this system having been developed at Crewe under John Ramsbottom. Thus equipped, one of these engines, No. 229, *Watt,* was able to make what was then a record length of non-stop run, 103¾ miles from Holyhead to Crewe, with a special carrying despatches in connection with the famous Trent dispute with the U.S.A. in 1862. Engines Nos. 667 *Marmion* and 806 *Waverley* on alternate days worked the 10 a.m. Edinburgh express between Euston and Crewe during the exciting Race to the North in 1888. In later years these little engines did a good deal of very useful work as pilots to heavy express trains requiring an assistant engine. Our picture shows one of these engines as originally built, without cab, and in the green livery of the L.N.W.R. standard until 1873.

24 **Sturrock 0-6-0 with Steam Tender;** Great Northern Railway.

Archibald Sturrock, who became Locomotive Superintendent of the G.N.R. in 1850, was one of the boldest and most original railway engineers of his day. He had scarcely taken up his appointment before he was designing engines with unusually large boilers, and he was constantly striving to get more power per unit of weight. He had every reason to do so with his heavy goods and mineral engines, because the coal traffic southwards from Yorkshire was going up by leaps and bounds. So, in conjunction with one of the biggest boilers seen in Great Britain up to time, he patented an arrangement whereby the tender constituted a separate engine, taking its steam from the one large boiler. The tender was, in fact, a second 0-6-0. The first trials of these engines were very successful. Between

London and Peterborough, where the orginary goods engines could take 30 loaded coal wagons, the big engines with the steam tenders took 45. On the level stretches of the Lincolnshire loop line the single-engine load could be increased from 35 wagons to 60. But the engines proved too powerful. They were ahead of their time, and when not used at full capacity they were not economic. Furthermore they were not liked by the men, who felt it was asking too much of them to look after what was virtually a double engine. Consequently maintenance was not good, and the bold experiment had to be abandoned, after no fewer than 50 steam tenders had been in service.

25 Conner 8 ft. Single; Caledonian Railway.

Before the Caledonian Railway was ever built extreme controversy raged over the proposal to carry the line up the glen of Evan Water from Beattock to an altitude of more than 1000 ft. above sea level. Such gradients were not considered practical; yet after the route was settled, to include one of the worst inclines to be found on any main line in Great Britain – 10 miles at 1 in 75 – the superintendent who presided over the locomotive department from 1856 to 1876, Benjamin Conner, adopted as standard the 2-2-2 type for express passenger work, and moreover with driving wheels of no less than 8 ft. 2 in. diameter. This might have seemed the reverse of suitability for such a steeply graded route; but the engines were beautifully designed, superbly constructed, and did their work well. The first two were built at St Rollox works, Glasgow, in 1859, and the engine illustrated in our picture belongs to a slightly later batch, albeit of the same general design. It is interesting to recall that three engines of this same design were built by Neilson and Co. of Glasgow for the Egyptian State Railways. On the Caledonian, despite the great increase in the weight and speed of trains since their first introduction, the Conner eight-footers remained on the crack trains till 1884–5, and the last of them was not withdrawn until 1901.

26 Great North of Scotland Railway; one of the earliest British 4-4-os designed by W. Cowan, 1865.

The 'Great North', to give it the usual abbreviated title, was a curious railway. Its first locomotive superintendent was Daniel Kinnear Clark, an engineer perhaps better known for his treatises on railway machinery than for his work on the G.N.S.R. He did most of his work from an office in London, more than 500 miles away from the nearest point on the railway! There was a tradition of quarrelling in the management of the railway at Aberdeen, and Clark resigned precipitately when certain directors criticized his work. W. Cowan took over the job in 1857, and he developed Clark's design practice, and put on the road a number of interesting and gaily finished locomotives. The engine chosen for illustration is one of the first of the 4-4-0 type ever to run in Great Britain. It was one of a batch of nine built by Robert Stephenson and Co. in 1862–4. These had the dome placed immediately over the firebox, and a good point in design was the raising of the firebox above the level of the top of the boiler barrel, so as to give additional steam space in the hottest part of the boiler. A curious feature was the outside framing of the four-wheeled tender, which in its shape rather gave the impression that a centre pair of wheels had been left out. These engines did excellent work, and some survived in service until 1920.

27 Kirtley's '800' Class; Midland Railway.

A great locomotive historian, the late E. L. Ahrons, once described these locomotives as 'one of the most celebrated classes of express engines that ever ran in this country'. Our picture shows one of them as originally built, and carrying the handsome green livery that preceded the famous 'Derby red'. They were fast, powerful engines, with boilers that steamed very freely; and the 48 engines of this class were the mainstay of the Anglo-Scottish express services of the Midland for many years. They had about five years in their original condition, and then S. W. Johnson, Kirtley's successor, modernized them, putting on larger boilers and larger cylinders. They were immensely popular with the drivers and firemen, and they were that extremely rare species – an engine that is thermally efficient and yet a real 'drivers' engine'. Many of the men declared that the harder you thrashed them the better and more sweetly they responded. For many years they worked turn and turn about with the larger and newer engines built after them. When Johnson modernized them he fitted his own type of boiler mountings, and decked them in 'Derby red'. In many ways they looked finer than ever. The majority of them were still running at the time of the grouping, and so passed into L.M.S.R. ownership after 50 years of service.

28 **Robert Sinclair's 2-2-2;** Great Eastern Railway.

These celebrated engines, of which there were 30, did all the most important express working on the Great Eastern Railway for nearly 20 years. Even for their own day they were, theoretically, not very powerful, having cylinders no larger than 16 in. diameter by 24 in. stroke. The boilers were small, and carried only 120 lb. per sq. in. pressure. Nevertheless they were beautifully designed and constructed machines and did much finer work than their small dimensions would suggest. No fewer than four different firms were concerned in their construction. The first five came from Fairbairn and Sons, of Manchester; then came 10 from the Avonside Engine Company, of Bristol, in

the year 1864. Next, in 1865, came another ten from Kitson's of Leeds, and the last five (1866–7) were built in France, by the celebrated firm Schneider et Cie, of Le Creusot – makers of the once-deadly 75 mm. gun used in large quantities by the French Army. These French-built engines were, by general consent of the drivers, the best of the entire stud. In their hey-day they were divided between the four 'crack' sheds, Stratford, Cambridge, Ipswich and Norwich; but after larger engines were put on to the principal trains the old Sinclair singles were transferred to the G.N. and G.E. Joint line for working between March and Doncaster. There they continued the good work for another dozen years. The last of them were not scrapped until 1894.

29 **A Stirling 8-footer;** Great Northern Railway.

It is no exaggeration to say that these engines, the first of which was built in 1870 at Doncaster, are among the most famous express passenger locomotives of all time. Engines of this class were built at intervals from 1870 until 1895 with gradually changing and improving features of constructional detail, but all alike in the extreme elegance of their external proportions. The long domeless boiler, the beautifully shaped safety valve casing, the majestic sweep of the running plate over the driving wheel centre immediately caught the eye; and as one came to examine one of these engines in more detail one realized the numerous touches of beauty and distinction put into them by a designer who was at one and the same time an artist and a master craftsman. The earlier engines of the class had the picturesque slotted splashers as exemplified by No. 5 in our picture. Later engines had them closed in, and the last batch of all, built in the year that Stirling died, had a rather more generous canopy in the cab roof. They were no mere ornaments. They ran the fastest express service in the world, during the 'eighties' of last century, and they climed the banks as well as they flew along at 70 to 75 m.p.h. on the downhill stretches. On the last night of the Race to the North, in 1895, engine No. 668 took the Aberdeen sleeping car train over the 105½ miles from Kings Cross to Grantham in 101 min. The pioneer engine of the class, No. 1, built in 1870, is preserved in the Railway Museum at York.

30 A Stroudley 'G' Class 2-2-2 'Petworth'; London Brighton and South Coast Railway.

William Stroudley, Locomotive Superintendent of the L.B.&S.C.R. from 1870 to 1889, developed a classic style in locomotive lineaments which, combined with the beautiful livery, made the Brighton engines unique for all time. But Stroudley was not merely an artist in styling and finish. His locomotives were soundly designed, superbly constructed and maintained, and very economical to run. Furthermore, he was ahead of most of his contemporaries in the degree to which all his engines incorporated standard parts and fittings. The 'G' class engines, of which 24 were built at Brighton during the years 1880–2, were the regular engines on the Portsmouth line. It is remarkable that Stroudley should have designed single-wheelers for that route, because it includes a good deal of sharp grading, and a distinctly stiff climb over the North Downs between Dorking and Horsham. Nevertheless these extremely pretty little engines did excellent work on this route for many years, and it was not until after 1895 that replacement of them commenced. They were nearly all named after beautiful country villages and resorts on the line, and in the Isle of Wight. A notable exception was No. 329, which was specially named *Stephenson*. As such it played a notable part in the Stephenson Centenary celebrations in Newcastle in 1881.

31 The Tay Bridge Engine; North British Railway.

The period was one in which the majority of railways in Great Britain were using six-wheeled passenger engines. The eight-wheelers were mostly 4-2-2. Engine No. 224 of the North British, with its sister engine No. 264, were the first of what became the most characteristic British passenger engine type of pre-grouping days, namely the 4-4-0 with inside cylinders, and inside frames throughout. They were big engines for the period, and apart from the unusual design of the boiler, with the dome over the firebox, they were also characterized by their solid bogie wheels. But if Nos. 224 and 264, were notable in conception and design No. 224 achieved a notoriety unique in British railway history. On the night of December 28, 1879, she was hauling the ill-fated train that entered upon the Tay Bridge at the moment that the high girders collapsed. Engine and train went down with the ruins of the bridge, and of the eighty persons on board there was not a single survivor. The engine, however, was the one thing that did survive the disaster. It lay for nearly four months at the bottom of the Firth of Tay, but was then recovered, and found to be so little damaged that it was taken to Cowlairs Works, Glasgow, for repair, travelling on its own wheels. After overhaul the engine went into service again, and lasted for another 39 years. It was eventually scrapped in 1919, just forty years after its plunge into the Firth of Tay.

32 '901' Class; North Eastern Railway.

Edward Fletcher was born and bred in the very cradle of the steam locomotive. He was serving his apprenticeship with George Stephenson at the time the *Rocket* was built, and he assisted in the trials at Killingworth Colliery, before that famous engine left for Liverpool, to win triumph and immortal engineering fame in the Rainhill trials. In 1854 he was appointed

Locomotive Superintendent of the North Eastern Railway and in that position he designed a host of striking and uniformly successful engines. There was no such thing as standardization in Fletcher's day. Engines were built to do individual jobs, and even when the close of his career was approaching and he produced, in the '901' class 2-4-0s, his masterpiece, there were numerous individual varieties. Some were built at Gateshead Works, others by contractors, and Fletcher allowed the latter to use their own standard types of boiler mounting and finish. But they were alike in being gorgeously arrayed, and the engine in our picture, No. 910, is today preserved and stands in the Railway Museum at York in all her original glory. Looking on No. 910 the visitor may well wonder what railways were like when locomotives were so gaily bedecked. But those elegant little engines hauled the Scotch expresses of their day, frequently attaining speeds of more than 70 m.p.h. They were very economical in working and immense favourites with their drivers and firemen.

33 David Jones's 'F' Class; Highland Railway.

From its inception the Highland Railway had used locomotives that were small in relation to the heavy gradients and hard work required in working over the 1484 ft. altitude of Drumochter summit, in the heart of the Grampian Mountains. Furthermore, though the company was served, from 1865 onwards, by engineers of high calibre, funds were not available for the purchase of larger and more suitable locomotives. By the year 1873, however, the position had changed, and David Jones was able to design and have built what was then one of the heaviest and most powerful passenger engines in Europe. A first order for 10 or these splendid machines was placed. The majority were named at first after counties through which the Highland Railway

ran, but others were named after personalities, and the country estates of directors and other gentlemen prominent in the management of the railway. Our picture shows the *Ardross*, named after the home of Sir Alexander Matheson, Chairman of the Company. The 'F' class embodied the heavy double-framing at the front-end that had been characteristic of Alexander Allan's designs whether at Crewe or in Scotland. This style was continued in later Jones engines on the Highland Railway for another eighteen years after the introduction of the 'F' class.

34 The 'Europa' Class; London, Chatham and Dover Railway.

In 1873 the Chatham Railway gained the exclusive contract for carrying the Royal Mail between London and Dover, and to ensure punctuality the Locomotive Superintendent, William Martley, was instructed to provide four new locomotives of enhanced power. Few engines of a small class have, in relation to their small numbers, gained praise or fame to a greater extent than these splendid little 2-4-0s, which were named *Europa*, *Asia*, *Africa* and *America*. They immediately became known as the 'Mail Engines', and became familiar and popular with the travelling public from their handsome appearance and excellent work. These trains stopped at Herne Hill, to attach or detach the City portions, and the 74 miles between Herne Hill and Dover Town were booked to be covered at an average speed of about 47 m.p.h. At the height of the Chatham Company's Continental mail traffic there were seven expresses daily booked to make an overall average speed of 44 m.p.h. between Victoria and Dover Pier. In 1873-8, the hey-day of the 'Europa' class, this was excellent going over a hilly road. They were fitted with new boilers in 1892 and survived to carry the gay S.E.&C.R. livery. In the present century they continued to be called upon for express work, and they were not finally withdrawn from traffic until 1907-8.

35 4-4-0 Tank Engine; North London Railway.

The North London, although originating as a protégé of the London and North Western, displayed a striking individuality so far as locomotive design was concerned. During mid-Victorian times it might indeed have seemed that the lowlier and dingier of the districts through which a railway ran the gayer and more ornate was the finish of the locomotive. The yellow Stroudley engines of the Brighton Railway worked through the Thames Tunnel, and these spanking little Adams 4-4-0 tanks worked around Canonbury, Islington, Dalston, and Poplar. If they are compared to their contemporaries on the Metropolitan and the Metropolitan District it will be realized how different in outward appearance it was possible to make a locomotive of the same wheel arrangement, of similar power, and capable of doing the same work! The gay livery was retained until 1882, when a change was made to the utilitarian 'black' of the London and North Western Railway. These pretty little 4-4-0 tanks were rebuilt in the 'eighties' to have cabs and more modern boiler mountings. Unlike the Metropolitan and the Metropolitan District Railways, the North London built their own locomotives, at Bow Works. In still later years some North London locomotives were overhauled at the Crewe works of the L.&N.W.R.

36 A 'Small Scotchman'; London, Chatham and Dover Railway.

The London, Chatham and Dover Railway was distinguished by the complexity and volume of its London suburban services; and these were not confined to its own metals. In its sustained drive to develop traffic it possessed running powers over the lines of several other companies, and in 1866 more powerful locomotives were needed to cope, particularly, with the services over the Great Northern and Midland lines. These L.C.D.R. trains originated at Moorgate, and ran to Wood Green and Hendon respectively. Another very important service was that between the Crystal Palace and the London termini. Martley introduced the smart and workmanlike little 0-4-2 tank engines illustrated here. Not only were they built in Scotland, by Neilson and Co., but for some reason these London suburban tank engines all had Scottish place names, ranging from islands off the West Coast, like *Iona*, *Bute*, and *Arran*, to famous rivers like *Spey*, *Tay*, and *Nith*. They all put in nearly forty years of hard work in and around London. By the time they came into S.E.&C.R. ownership, and duly carried the new livery, they had been reboilered and so exchanged their picturesque, distinctive look, shown in our picture, for a more conventional domed boiler.

37 The Steam Inner Circle; Metropolitan Railway.

These famous engines, the first to be owned by the Metropolitan Railway, were not ready in time for the opening of the line in 1863. At that time the extent of this pioneer Underground railway in London was only from a junction with the Great Western at Bishops Road (Paddington) to Farringdon Street. The line was worked first by the Great Western, and later by the Great Northern Railway until the Metropolitan 4-4-0 tanks arrived. These latter were splendid engines and worked the Underground services without intermission until the Inner Circle was electrified in 1906. As originally built they had the characteristic features of Beyer-Peacock & Co. in the huge bell-mouthed domes, placed cheek-by-jowl with the chimney. The bogie had an exceptionally short wheelbase; the cylinders were steeply inclined, and they had no cabs.

Today it certainly takes a stretch of the imagination to picture what travelling on the Inner Circle was like, in steam days! Our picture shows one of these engines in their later form, with a more modern boiler, and the handsome livery of Metropolitan steam locomotives at the time when the inner-London sections of the line were electrified. One of these historic locomotives has been preserved, and is to be seen in the Transport Museum at Clapham.

38 2-4-0 tank for the Underground lines; Great Western Railway.

These delightful little engines were introduced to work the London suburban trains of the G.W.R., and particularly to work through the Underground lines of the Metropolitan Railway Inner Circle, to Liverpool Street. Engine No. 968, which is the subject of our picture, was one of the fourth batch, being built at Swindon in 1874. So successful were they in hauling the smartly-timed business trains that construction of them continued for 30 years after their first introduction. The later engines of the class had small cabs, but the majority had nothing more than weatherboards. In any case the cabe provided shelter only when they werr running chimney first. They were neves turned at journey's end though, and when running bunker first, which represented half their weekly mileage the men were quite exposed to the weather. No fewer than 110 of them were built, and the majority had large condensing pipes shown in our picture. When running over the Metropolitan line they were not allowed to exhaust their steam in the normal way, to minimize the effect of steam working in the tunnels. The exhaust steam was turned instead into the side tanks. Many of them were still at work in the London area in the late nineteen-twenties, but by that time they were painted plain green, without lining, and with black underframes.

39 Dean's Standard Gauge 2-2-2; for the Great Western.

While the broad gauge was still in existence provision had nevertheless to be made for the standard-gauge parts of the line, and of these none was more important than that to Birmingham, Chester and Birkenhead. Daniel Gooch had designed a class of ten 2-2-2s, with the usual sandwich frames, in 1861, and Dean thoroughly modernized these engines in 1877, giving them larger cylinders, but at first retaining a domeless boiler. They worked in the same link as the Armstrong 'Sir Alexander' class, which had the more conventional plate frames, and in due course their appearance was still further modernized by the closing in of their open splashers, and the fitting of new domed boilers. Our picture shows one of these engines as running about 1900. They were very fast and free-running engines, and did splendid work on the Paddington–Birmingham expresses, all of which at that time ran via Oxford. The drivers showed great skill in getting them away from a stop without excessive slipping, and they took loads of 300 tons, and sometimes more, with complete success. The form shown in our picture did not represent their final form. In the twentieth century some of them were fitted with the new type of Swindon domeless boiler, and high Belpaire fireboxes. In this form they outlasted the larger Dean 4-2-2 express engines, and No. 165 of the '157' class was the last single-driver locomotive to remain in regular service on the G.W.R. She was not withdrawn until 1915.

40 Webb's 'Precedent' Class 2-4-0; London and North Western Railway.

The 'Precedent' class was a development of John Ramsbottom's 'Newton' class of 2-4-0; but the improvements made by Webb extended to much more than the provision of larger cylinders, a larger boiler, and higher boiler pressure. The 'Precedents' were among the first locomotives in Britain – probably in the world – in which the arrangements for steam flow were made very short, and direct, with the result that these little engines developed power and speed out of all proportion to their size, and generally in advance of engines of the same wheel arrangement on which the cylinder and valve layout were more conventional – and at that time involved circuitous passages and ports. In the eighteen-nineties engine No. 2002 *Madge* of this class attained the high speed of 88 m.p.h., while during the Race to the North, in 1895, No. 790 *Hardwicke* ran the racing portion of the Euston–Aberdeen Tourist express over the 141.1 miles from Crewe to Carlisle at an average speed of 67 m.p.h. The engine illustrated, No. 2191 *Snowdon* was the last of the class to remain in regular passenger service, and was not withdrawn until 1932.

41 **James Stirling's 4-4-0 of 1873;**
Glasgow and South Western Railway.
For 25 years, from 1853 to 1878 there was a Stirling in the chair at Kilmarnock Works. Until 1866 it was Patrick, who then left to attain great eminence as the locomotive engineer of the Great Northern Railway. He was succeeded, on the G.& S.W.R. by his younger brother James, who continued the family tradition in that he built no locomotives other than with domeless boilers. In other respects he differed from his brother, particularly in the matter of coupling the driving wheels. Patrick to the very end of his long life never built a coupled engine for express passenger work. James Stirling not only built 4-coupled engines, but in 1873 put the Glasgow and South Western Railway in the forefront of British locomotive practice with the very fine 4-4-0 express engine illustrated in our picture. One engine only was built in 1873; but when the design was proved construction continued until 1877, by which time there were 22 of them on the road. They were

very large and imposing engines for their day, and included one innovation of detail, in James Stirling's steam-operated reversing gear. Hitherto all engines had a manually operated gear, which was often very hard to move – this being before the days of ball-bearings and other friction-reducing devices. The Stirling 4-4-0s ran the Midland Scotch expresses between Carlisle and Glasgow, from 1876 onwards, and they were among the fastest trains in the country at that time.

42 **Dugald Drummond's N.B.R. 4-4-0 of 1876.**
The year 1876 saw the opening of the Midland Railway Company's independent route to Carlisle – the far-famed Settle and Carlisle line – and through services were inaugurated from St Pancras to both Edinburgh and Glasgow. In the running of the former service the North British Railway was in partnership with the Midland, and for the new accelerated services, in keen competition with the established routes to Kings Cross and to Euston, some powerful new locomotives were put on the road. Known as the '476', or 'Waverley' class, they were the first of a remarkable series of 4-4-0 locomotives designed by Dugald Drummond, and his younger brother, Peter. Technically they were notable for the length of the coupling rods, namely 9 ft., which was most unusual at that time. Drummond developed the type in later years on the Caledonian and then on the London and South Western Railway, while his brother took the design to the Highland, and then to the Glasgow and South Western. Drummond was an earnest follower of Stroudley's practice, having worked under him at Brighton, and he took to the North British the practice of naming locomotives after the stations they served on the line. Ten out of the twelve engines of the '476' class were named after places on the 'Waverley' route, between Edinburgh and Carlisle.

43 A Caley 'Jumbo'; Drummond 0-6-0.

A great change came over the locomotive practice of the Caledonian Railway when Dugald Drummond was appointed superintendent in 1882. Until then practically all the locomotives, passenger and goods alike, had been fitted with outside cylinders, carrying on the traditions established in Scotland by Alexander Allan when he came north from the L.&N.W.R. at Crewe. But Drummond, following his success on the North British Railway, used a very much neater and more modern design, and the smart 0-6-0 goods engine, first introduced in 1884, was typical of his earlier work on the Caledonian. They proved splendid engines, not only for goods but for general service all over the line, and formed the basis of goods engine development at St Rollox for many years subsequently. Not only this: Dugald Drummond took the design with him to the London and South Western Railway, while his younger brother Peter adopted it, in almost exactly the same form, on the Highland Railway. In later years in Scotland the 'Caley Jumbos' could be seen doing all kinds of light and intermediate duty, and in years just before World War II they were frequently used for assisting heavy express passenger trains over the very severe gradients of the Callander and Oban Railway. At that time, painted in the L.M.S. plain black, it was difficult to distinguish the Caledonian and Highland varieties of the design, except by the numbers.

44 Webb's Standard Coal Engine; London and North Western Railway.

The L.&N.W.R. was well-known at one time as the largest joint-stock corporation in the world. Its princely revenue was derived very largely from its goods and mineral traffic, and the first new engine design of Francis W. Webb, after his taking office as Chief Mechanical Engineer in 1871, was an excellent 0-6-0 for heavy goods traffic. In later years the idea of a small 0-6-0, with cylinders no larger than 17 in. diameter by 24 in. stroke doing 'heavy' work would seem strange ; but at the time of their first introduction, in 1873, the '17 inch coal engines', as they were always known, were among the most powerful freight engines in the country. They were extremely simple, in both design and construction, and very cheap and easy to build. As an experiment Webb set Crewe works a test to see how quickly one of these engines could be built. The result could be described as sensational, for the engine was built and left the erecting shop under her own steam in 25½ hours! This class was an L.&N.W.R. standard, and construction of them continued for 19 years (1873–92). Eventually there were no fewer than 500 of them at work. During this time there were no changes in design. Those built in 1892 were exactly the same as those of the first batch of 1873 – a striking tribute to the effectiveness of the original design. No fewer than 227 out of the original 500 were still in service in 1923, when the L.&N.W.R. passed into the London Midland and Scottish system.

45 The Dean 'Goods'; G.W.R.

This class, of which 280 were built in the years 1883–1898, proved to be perhaps the most notable design using the very common 0-6-0 wheel arrangement, ever to run in Great Britain. At the time of its first appearance something of a surprise was created in that it was the first Great Western engine design to have only inside frames. Hitherto outside frames, mostly using the sandwich form of construction had been universal. The first 20 engines of the class had domeless boilers; but after several batches there came the familiar huge polished brass dome, and the usual accompaniments of decoration characteristic of the Dean period, and applied alike to goods and passenger engines. At first, of course, the engines were non-superheated, but in more recent years new superheated boilers have been fitted to many of them, and they have done remarkable work on the light and branch passenger trains, as well as in the haulage of goods. Many of them saw service overseas during the First World War, both in France, and in the Middle East, while during the Second World War no fewer than 109 of these veterans were requisitioned for war work. An engine of this class has been preserved, and is housed in the G.W.R. Museum at Swindon.

46 A 'Skye Bogie'; Highland Railway.

The original of the 'F' class passenger engines, shown in Plate 33, can be traced to a reconstruction of one of the earlier 2-4-0s made by David Jones in 1873. The Dingwall and Skye line, crossing the county of Ross, to reach the west coast, involved some exceedingly severe railway working with gradients steeper than anywhere else on the Highland system, and incessantly sharp curvature. To render the 2-4-0s already available more suited to these conditions Jones rebuilt one of them with a leading bogie. This engine was so successful that the bogie type was adopted for the Class 'F' main line passenger engines of 1874, and following this some similar engines, but with small coupled wheels, were built at Inverness specially for the Dingwall and Skye line. These proved to be remarkably handy and efficient engines, and some of them put in more than 40 years' service on the line. When originally introduced they carried the gay livery characteristic of all Highland engines, passenger and goods; but they were most familiar in their plain green of later years. They were the first Highland engines not to carry names. They did all the work over the very hilly and winding route to the Kyle of Lochalsh – passenger, goods and cattle alike. The men became so attached to them that when larger engines were eventually put on to the Dingwall and Skye line they were at first regarded as clumsy and unnecessarily big!

47 Midland Railway; A Johnson 2-4-0.

Samuel Waite Johnson was one of the supreme artists of the locomotive engineering world. He designed engines that were simple, workmanlike, and efficient in traffic, yet having a beauty of 'line' that has never been surpassed. Every detail was perfectly proportioned, and one can see this in the handsomely-shaped chimney, the curves of the dome and of the brass safety valve casing. His earliest passenger engines were of the 2-4-0 type, after which he built 4-4-0s. But for general service on the Midland Railway he built further batches of the 2-4-0 type from 1879 onwards, and it is one of these that has been chosen to illustrate his earlier work. No. 1400 was the first of a batch of ten engines built at Derby in 1879, and painted in the light green colour then standard. The magnificent crimson-lake, 'Derby-red', of later Midland engines was introduced by Johnson some years later. The '1400' class engines were at first put on to the London–Leeds route, but after four years the entire ten of them were transferred to Lancaster and Carnforth sheds to run the important expresses between Leeds, Bradford and Morecambe on the one hand, and the connecting trains to the Furness Railway on the other. On this duty the ten engines put in 40 years of service, and even after displacement from those duties they continued in secondary service for many years afterwards.

48 The 'Gladstone'.

This was the first engine of the most celebrated of all Stroudley's designs. It was built at Brighton in 1882, but engines of this class continued to be built at intervals down to the year 1891, by which time 36 of them were at work. The outstanding feature of these engines – designed for the fastest and heaviest traffic on the line – was the wheel arrangement, namely the 0-4-2. Engineers of other railways looked askance at the use of large diameter driving wheels (6 ft. 6 in.) at the leading end of an engine intended to run fast; but the 'Gladstones' proved very steady and smooth riding machines, with a gentle easy ride at speed. They proved exceptionally powerful for their size, and the the way they would start away from Victoria station, and take a heavy train up the 1 in 64 gradient on to the Grosvenor Road Bridge frequently confounded their critics. The pioneer engine has been restored to its original form, and its gorgeous colouring, and is now to be seen in the Railway Museum at York. It was withdrawn from service in 1927, after 45 years of hard work on the Brighton line.

49 **Charles Sacré's 2-2-2;** Manchester, Sheffield and Lincolnshire Railway.
The M.S.&L. was a curious and difficult system for which to provide locomotive power. It included the level lines east of Sheffield which ran across the Lincolnshire plains, and there were the relatively easy sections of the Cheshire Lines Committee, west of Manchester. But between these two groups was the very severe connecting line over the Pennines, between Sheffield and Manchester. Over this latter route the M.S.&L. were partners with the Great Northern in operating a fast and highly competitive through service between Manchester and Kings Cross, against the rival services of the London and North Western and the Midland. Although Charles Sacré had built a number of 4-4-0 locomotives from 1878 onwards, it was in 1883 that he turned out from Gorton Works the beautiful series of 7 ft. 6 in. 2-2-2s of which one is illustrated in our picture. These were clearly intended to make the best of both

worlds, and some of them were put to work on the Manchester–Liverpool and Manchester–Southport services of the C.L.C. while others were reserved for the Great Northern through expresses to Kings Cross. On these trains the M.S.&L. engines worked through between Manchester and Grantham, thus running for 33 miles over the Great Northern main line.

50 **South Eastern Railway 'F' Class.**
James Stirling was one of the earliest exponents of the practice of locomotive standardization, and during his tenure of office as Locomotive Superintendent at Ashford, from 1878 to 1898, he introduced no more than six classes, and three were relatively small in numbers. His three principal classes, 0-6-0 for goods, 0-4-4 tank for suburban passenger, and 4-4-0 for express passenger were built in relatively large numbers, and totalled eventually 122, 118, and 88 respectively. The 'F' class express passenger, illustrated here, was typical of James Stirling's style. They were striking rather than handsome; but they did some excellent work on the road, and they continued on main line work long after the newer engines of Wainwright's design had been introduced. James Stirling, like his elder brother Patrick on the Great Northern Railway, built no engines for the South Eastern Railway other than with domeless boilers. They steamed well, despite relatively poor fuel. Speed on the South Eastern was limited, by permanent way restrictions, to a maximum of 60 m.p.h. over the entire system, and so the highly competitive boat train services, to and from Dover, on which the S.E.R. was continually up against the enterprise of the London, Chatham and Dover Railway, had to be maintained by hard running, uphill. The 'F' class engines excelled in this respect. Two of them put in no less than 44 years' service.

51 **Metropolitan District Railway;** a Beyer-Peacock 4-4-0 tank.

These engines were generally of the same design as those of the Metropolitan Railway, and our picture shows one of them in a very early form. In view of the way the two companies eventually became inter-connected on the Underground lines in Central London, and worked various services jointly, the actual ownership of the tracks may be mentioned. The 'District' owned the line from Earls Court over the south side of the Inner Circle, to Aldgate East and Whitechapel while the Metropolitan extended from Edgware Road to Gloucester Road, at the western end, and to Aldgate and Minories Junction at the eastern end. The Inner Circle in steam days was worked jointly, some trains by District and some by Metropolitan engines and stock in proportions equal to the respective mileages owned by each company. It worked out that *all* trains going clockwise round the Circle were Metropolitan and the majority going anti-clockwise were District. The District Railway had westward and south-westward extensions from Earls Court, to Richmond, Ealing, Hounslow, and Wimbledon. All these trains were worked by the 4-4-0 tank engines of which a total of 54 were built for the District Railway, between 1871 and 1886. They 'saw steam out' on the District, and with the 66 similar engines of the Metropolitan represented a remarkably efficient, if not very handsome stud.

52 **London Tilbury and Southend Railway;** an Adams 4-4-2 tank engine.

These engines, of which there were 36 in all, were designed by W. Adams, while he was Locomotive Superintendent of the Great Eastern Railway. They originally had very severe-looking stove-pipe chimneys, but were later modified to the handsome appearance shown in our picture. The first batch, built by Sharp, Stewart and Co. of Manchester, came south in charge of a young engineer named Thomas Whitelegg, who was later appointed superintendent of the L.T.&S.R., and was later succeeded in that office by his son, Robert. The Whiteleggs, father and son, had a great regard for handsome appearance in a locomotive, and successive enlargements of the basic 4-4-2 design enhanced rather than detracted from their graceful lines. All engines of the L.T.&S.R. were named after stations on the line, and while there was a certain distinction in names like *Southend*, *Shoeburyness*, *Upminster*, *Purfleet*, and the like, things became a little less interesting when locomotives were named after dingy places in the London suburban area such as *Whitechapel*, *Black Horse Road*, and *Commercial Road*. These engines lasted well into the L.M.S. era. The first of them was not scrapped until 1930, and the last was not withdrawn until October 1935.

53 **North London Railway;** an Adams 4-4-0 tank of 1868.

William Adams was one of the many locomotive engineers of Victorian times who moved rapidly from one railway to another. Examples of his fine work were eventually to be found not only on the North London, but also on the Great Eastern, on the London, Tilbury and Southend, and most distinguished of all, on the London and South Western. Generally he favoured outside cylinders and his 4-4-0 tank design for the North London was originally turned out in the same brilliant and ornate style as the inside cylinder 4-4-0 (see reference 35). This style of painting was continued on the North London Railway until 1882, after which a livery corresponding closely to that of the London and North Western Railway was adopted. It is in this form that the Adams 4-4-0 tank is illustrated. It was in such form that these powerful and efficient little engines became familiar to thousands of season-ticket holders travelling to and from the City terminus at Broad Street. They worked trains of little four-wheeled coaches, seemingly of caravan length, over the Great Northern main line to Potters Bar, and to High Barnet over a steeply graded branch. They were familiar on this duty well into the nineteen-twenties. On these trains they carried the destination on a huge board that extended almost to the full width of the buffer beam.

54 Maryport and Carlisle Railway; a 2-4-0 passenger engine.

The Maryport and Carlisle Railway was one of the most consistently properous of all the local railways in Great Britain. It served the northern part of the West Cumberland coalfield, and carried the coals to Carlisle. From 1859 onwards until the fateful year of 1914 it never paid a dividend of less than $5\frac{1}{4}$ per cent. Yet prosperity never went to the head of its astute management. There was no heavy capital expenditure on new works, or locomotives built for prestige purposes, and the example chosen for illustration in this book is a picturesque little thing added to the stock in 1867 but still retained in service until 1921. The engine R1 could not be classed as typical of the Maryport and Carlisle Railway, because there was nothing that could be called a standard design, or representative of standard practice. Locomotives were added to the stock in ones and twos, as required; and the earlier ones were carefully repaired and kept going. The smart green engines were familiar sights at Carlisle, and there was a time when it was a regular thing for the Maryport company to work the evening mail train southwards over the Furness Line. The bright green turnout made a strong contrast to the iron-ore red of the Furness locomotives, and was nevertheless an excellent travelling ambassador of one of the best-run small railways in the country.

55 Matthew Holmes's 4-4-0; North British Railway.

In 1890 the Forth Bridge was opened, and the North British Railway was immediately able to provide very much faster services from Edinburgh to Perth, on the one hand, and on the East Coast main line to Aberdeen. To provide suitable engine power for the new trains Matthew Holmes built a very much enlarged version of the Drummond 4-4-0s of the 'Waverley' class, with much larger boilers and cylinders. Externally they could be distinguished by the neat, lock-up safety valves on the dome, and by the style of cab, which followed that of Patrick Stirling, on the Great Northern Railway at Doncaster. The North British was fortunate in having such excellent engines when the time came for the great Race to the North in the summer of 1895. Then the 8 p.m. Tourist express from Kings Cross to Aberdeen was worked at ever increasing speed, until the final night of the race the $59\frac{1}{4}$ miles from Edinburgh to Dundee were covered in 59 min. In view of the incessant curvature of the line and of the stiff gradients this was a performance that can only be called venturesome, in the speeds at which many of the curves were taken. In normal working 80 min. was considered a fast time for this very awkward stretch of line; and to cut 20 minutes off this time was a marvellous tribute to Holmes's 4-4-0 locomotives and their crews.

56 James Holden's 7 ft. 2-2-2; Great Eastern Railway.

The existence of so many level stretches of line in Cambridge and Lincolnshire might suggest that the Great Eastern was an ideal line for single-driver locomotives. Actually the main line includes a number of sharp and severe gradients, not excepting the immediate start out of Liverpool Street up the 1 in 70 gradient of Bethnal Green bank. James Holden built 2-4-0 and 2-2-2 express locomotives of otherwise identical design with 7 ft. wheels, 18 in. by 24 in. cylinders and the same design of boiler. The 'singles' illustrated were exceptionally good engines in starting away, and taking quite heavy loads at the schedule speed demanded in the 1890s. These engines were used turn and turn about with the 2-4-0s of the 'T.19' class; but it was a time of quite rapid increase in train loads, and James Holden was soon required to build still larger engines. These '1000' class single-wheelers followed the precedent of the old Sinclairs, and went north for working on the Joint Line. Those stationed at Ely ran to York and back every day. Two of them were stationed at Harwich Parkeston Quay, and each of these ran to York with the North Country boat trains. At one time some of them were equipped for oil firing. Unfortunately the rapid advance in haulage requirements on the Great Eastern made larger locomotives necessary, and they were superseded sooner than their excellent performance really justified.

57 Lancashire and Yorkshire Railway; an Aspinall 4-4-0 of 1891.

For the greater part of the nineteenth century the Lancashire and Yorkshire was a slow, and generally rather shocking railway. But by the late 'eighties' there was a tremendous drive for all-round improvement and with the appointment of John A. F. Aspinall as Locomotive Superintendent some first-class engines were provided to run the vastly improved train services. The new 4-4-0 locomotives of 1891, built at Horwich works, were very speedy and reliable engines. They worked all over the system, as can be appreciated by the many depots at which they were stationed, namely Blackpool; Bolton; Fleetwood; Lostock Hall (Preston); Low Moor (Bradford); Newton Heath (Manchester); Sandhills (Liverpool); Southport; and Wakefield. They were the first real express locomotives that the Lancashire and Yorkshire Rail-

way have ever owned, and they worked the famous 'Club' trains from Manchester to Blackpool and Southport; the cross-country expresses to Leeds; and the very fast inter-city services between Liverpool and Manchester. The latter trains had to cover the 36 miles between the two cities in 40 minutes, non-stop, and although the bulk of the trains consisted of no more than three coaches it needed very smart running. Although finished in black, these engines were always very smartly kept, with the fine coat of arms of the company, including the red and white roses of Lancashire and Yorkshire, on the leading driving wheel splasher.

58 W. Adams's Jubilee Class; London and South Western.

These celebrated engines, of which no fewer than 90 were built between the years 1887 and 1895, were designed for fast mixed traffic duties – excursions, troop trains, and fast goods. They were unique on the L.&S.W.R. in having the 0-4-2 wheel arrangement, and the fact that they followed so soon after the famous 'Gladstones' of the L.B.&S.C.R. suggests that Adams derived the idea of them from Stroudley. The cylinders were the same on both classes, namely 18 in. diameter by 26 in. stroke and both had the steam chests beneath the cylinders. The 'Jubilees' had 6 ft. coupled wheels. But though so similar in their capacity and alike in their excellent performance on the road they were as unlike as any two engine classes could be in their outward appearance. The 'Jubilees' with their stove-pipe chimneys, plain domes, massive splashers, and cabs tended to look altogether bigger engines than the *Gladstones*. They were nevertheless beautifully finished in the handsome pale green of the L.&S.W.R. But for the onset of the Second World War they would all have been withdrawn by the end of 1939, after lives of more than 40 years. A number of them were, however, restored to traffic for the duration of the emergency, and the last three were not scrapped until 1948. These engines, Nos. 618, 627 and 636, were all between 55 and 56 years old at that time.

59 Worsdell-Von Borries 'J' Class.

During his distinguished career as Locomotive Superintendent of the North Eastern Railway T. W. Worsdell developed the Von Borries system of compounding, using only two cylinders of different sizes, and both placed inside the frames. The low pressure cylinders were large, and on the biggest engines of the type built at Gateshead Works the valve chests were outside. The 'J' class 4-2-2s were the culminating point of this development. They had driving wheels of 7 ft. 7 in. diameter, and were designed to haul heavy trains at high speed. This was in anticipation of increased traffic following the opening of the Forth Bridge in 1890. Although the North Eastern locomotives worked no farther north than Edinburgh they would be conveying the traffic for the new shortened routes to Perth, Inverness and Aberdeen. They proved to be among the fastest engines of their day. One of them was recorded at 90 m.p.h. with a load of 18 six-wheeled coaches; another of them ran a train of 32 coaches (six-wheelers) from Newcastle to Berwick, 67 miles in 78 minutes. This was remarkable work in 1889–90. Unfortunately mechanical troubles developed, and when Worsdell's younger brother Wilson took charge of the locomotive department he altered these engines to two-cylinder simples. As such they did nearly 30 more years of excellent work on the line.

60 Midland Railway; A Johnson 4-4-0.

By the 'nineties' of last century Johnson's artistry in locomotive design was reaching its zenith in successive batches of 4-4-0 express passenger engines. These hand-some machines all had the same general appearance, though there were variations in major dimensions and detail according to the different sections of the Midland Railway over which the engine had to run. Johnson had to provide for such diverse conditions as the mountain lines through the Peak District and among the Pennines; the fast stretches of the main line to London, and the long level roads in Lincolnshire. The 4-4-0s of whatever batch worked uniformly well, and the most recent of them, built about the turn of the century, performed feats of speed and load haulage that might well be thought scarcely possible from such slender looking engines. The example illustrated in our picture dates from 1892, and it was one of those with 7 ft. diameter coupled wheels, intended for the fastest stretches of the line. A feature of these engines, exemplifying Johnson's attention to neat and harmonious detail, is the flush-fitting smokebox door, with no visible fastening other than the central handle. The sweeping curves of the splashers over the driving wheels were another characteristic of all Johnson's 4-4-0 locomotives up to 1900.

61 The 'Adriatic'; London and North Western.

The 'Teutonic' class compounds represented the third development of Webb's three-cylinder compound system, in which there were two high pressure cylinders outside, and a single, very large low pressure inside. The earlier engines of this series, known respectively as the 'Experiment' and 'Dreadnought' classes, were inclined to be sluggish in running, through defects in their valve gear. But the 'Teutonic' had a single loose eccentric for the low pressure cylinder, and in conjunction with a better design of valves it made all the difference. Although they were uncertain starters, the 'Teutonics', once under way, were fast and powerful engines. No. 1304 *Jeanie Deans* worked the

2 p.m. Scottish corridor express, between Euston and Crewe for a period of more than 9 years, every day of the week, while No. 1309 *Adriatic* made the running between Euston and Crewe on the last night of the Race to the North in 1895 when the entire 540 miles from London to Aberdeen was covered in 512 min. The share of the *Adriatic* was to run the 158 miles from Euston to Crewe at an average speed of 64½ m.p.h. Another spectacular run was that of No. 1305 *Ionic*, which ran non-stop over the 299 miles from Euston to Carlisle with a special train, in 1895. At the time this was the longest non-stop run that had ever been made anywhere in the world. Nevertheless the 'Teutonics' did not last long after Webb's retirement in 1903. Their uncertain starting could not be tolerated in twentieth-century traffic conditions.

62 **Caledonian Railway;** one of the Drummond 4-4-0s.

Dugald Drummond, though a Scot by birth, education and early training, served some of the most impressionable years of his career under that early master of locomotive design, William Stroudley. He was in fact Works Manager at Brighton during those great years when the traditions of standardization and fine workmanship were being built up. When Drummond got his first independent appointment, that of Locomotive Superintendent of the North British Railway in 1875, he at once showed his appreciation of Stroudley's precepts, incorporated however in a locomotive type suited to Scottish needs, with the 4-4-0 wheel arrangement (reference 42). This design he used again, in a more highly developed form on the Caledonian, in the '66' class, first introduced in 1884. The East Coast companies were to learn to their discomfiture of the speedworthiness of these engines during the Race to the North in 1895, when several of the Drummond engines made remarkable records. Engine

No. 90, for example, ran from Carlisle to Perth, 150 miles non-stop at an average speed of 60 m.p.h., and at a time when 60 m.p.h. was the generally acknowledged speed of a British express train on level track these engines showed that they could run at 75 m.p.h. on the level between Perth and Forfar.

63 **A Dean 7 ft. 8 in. 4-2-2;** Great Western.

In these beautiful engines the cult for high finish and extensive ornamentation on Great Western locomotives seemed to reach its climax. There were many smaller 'singles' that were decorated in much the same style; but these engines reached the stage shown in our picture by a rapid process of evolution. The first examples were built at the time when the broad gauge was still in existence, and any new locomotives had to be designed with conversion from 7 ft. to 4 ft. 8½ in. gauge in view. With temporary running plates, and completely exposed driving wheels they looked positively ugly. Then came the narrow gauge 2-2-2 stage, which might have persisted had it not been for an alarming derailment of one of them in the Box Tunnel. In their final Dean stage, as depicted here, they did some splendid work on the long non-stop runs then worked on the G.W.R. There were 80 of them in all, and their usual runs were between Paddington and Newton Abbot, via Bristol; Paddington and Newport; and Paddington and Wolverhampton, the latter via either Banbury, or Worcester. Engine No. 3065 *Duke of Connaught* took part in the record run of the Ocean Mail from Plymouth to Paddington on May 9, 1904. The share of the Dean 'single' was to run the 118 miles from Bristol to Paddington in 99½ minutes – a wonderful achievement for that period.

64 **Glasgow and South Western Railway;** one of James Manson's 4-4-0s. Manson came to Kilmarnock in 1891,

having previously been Locomotive Superintendent of the Great North of Scotland Railway. He could be described as one of the most 'orthodox' of nineteenth-century Scottish locomotive engineers, relying upon the most simple and straightforward of designs, with the features most generally adopted at that time. Nevertheless, because of the essentially sound design of the detail parts, and of the care taken in maintaining the locomotives, his otherwise 'ordinary' 4-4-0s achieved an extremely high reputation. They were by no means nursed, or 'petted'. The Glasgow and South Western drivers of those days – particularly those on the Clyde coast and Stranraer trains – were very hard runners, and the engines had to stand up to the pounding of drivers who made it a point of honour to run their trains to time. On the main line from Glasgow to Carlisle rather different techniques prevailed. The distances run between stops were much longer, and the men were inclined to take their engines easily up the banks to save coal, and then to run as fast as they could downhill, on a light rein. But whatever the treatment – whether the 'coal-dodging' on the Carlisle road, or the pounding to Ayr and Stranraer – the Manson 4-4-0s of 1892 won golden opinions everywhere.

65 A North Eastern 'Rail Crusher'.

There was a time, during the 'eighties' of last century when it seemed as though the North Eastern Railway was becoming as thorough-going a compound line as the London and North Western, with T. W. Worsdell building many locomotives, passenger, goods and tank alike, on the two-cylinder Worsdell Von Borries system. But as soon as his younger brother took over there was a change, and the 'M' class 4-4-0 locomotives, built at Gateshead in 1893, were two-cylinder simples, fitted with W. M. Smith's piston valves. At the time of their construction they were the heaviest express passenger engines in the country, and were nicknamed the 'rail crushers' on that account. But they were far from being clumsy or ponderous engines. They rode with the ease and buoyancy of a swing; they were extremely fast, and it was largely due to their use that the North Eastern Railway was able to play such a notable part in the Race to the North, in 1895. There was one memorable night, indeed, when engine No. 1620 took the Aberdeen sleeping car express, weighing 100 tons behind the tender, from Newcastle to Edinburgh, 124½ miles, in 113 minutes. A feature of these engines, and in fact of all N.E.R. engines of the period, was the elegance of the cab interiors. Not only were all the metal fittings kept beautifully, but the sheet metal of the cab walls and sides was covered with a wood lining, which was always kept well polished.

66 A Johnston 'Spinner'; Midland 4-2-2.

These beautiful engines represent a remarkable, if passing phase in the history of the British steam locomotive. Since he took office in Derby in 1874, Johnson had built none save coupled engines, 2-4-0 and 4-4-0 for express passenger work, until the year 1887. In that year five express engines of the 4-2-2 type, with a single pair of driving wheels 7 ft. 4 in. diameter, were built at Derby. This revival of the obsolescent 'single wheeler' was due to the invention of the steam sanding gear, which by sanding the rails allowed engines to get a better grip. Once this was done Johnson was glad enough to revert to the simplicity and speediness of a 'single-wheeler' for the fastest duties. Between 1887 and 1900 no fewer than 90 new locomotives of the 4-2-2 type were built at Derby, of gradually increasing dimensions. They were most graciously proportioned engines and could run extremely fast. Speeds up to 90 m.p.h. were recorded with them. Though they were great favourites with the men, because of their smooth action and low coal consumption, they needed care in starting, with heavy trains, despite the use of steam sanding. The driving wheels would slip imperceptibly, without any of the clatter experienced on the footplate when a coupled engine slips; and for this reason they got their nickname of the 'Spinners'.

67 London and South Western Railway; an Adams 4-4-0.

The engine illustrated is one of a family of locomotives that were among the most powerful in the world at the time of their construction, and which by skilful design, and by superb workmanship put into them were amongst the most economical. Adams certainly did not turn his back upon compounding as a possible means of increased efficiency, and one of the Crewe-built Webb three-cylinder machines was tried on the L.&S.W.R. But Adams secured greater efficiency, and incomparably greater reliability by careful consideration in every stage of the circuit of the steam, from the regulator to the cylinders, and through the exhaust ports to the blast pipe and chimney; and the result was a free-running trouble-free engine. Externally these big 4-4-os, whether of the 6 ft. 7 in. or of the 7 ft. varieties, had a style of their own that was striking, and tremendously impressive at the time of their construction. A stovepipe chimney may seem the very antithesis of handsome design; but it set these locomotives off to perfection – so much so that when Dugald Drummond, who succeeded Adams, replaced them by shapely chimneys in his own style much of the striking character of the Adams 4-4-0 disappeared.

68 A Dunalastair 4-4-0; Caledonian Railway.

Splendid though the work of the Drummond 4-4-os had been it must be admitted that most of their spectacular running had been made with light trains. Traffic over the Anglo-Scottish routes was very much on the increase in the year of the Race, and the new Caledonian Locomotive Superintendent, John F. McIntosh, found it necessary to provide engines of far greater power. He took the Drummond 4-4-0, therefore, as a basis, and built on to it a very much larger boiler. Thus while the Drummonds had to be handled on 'a light rein' or else they would run short of steam, the new McIntosh engines could be worked hard for hours on end, if need be. The first of them, built at St Rollox Works in 1896, was named *Dunalastair* after the Highland home of the Caledonian Railway Chairman, and it can be said without exaggeration that no British locomotive class, of any period, has achieved greater fame. They proved themselves capable of running just as fast, and climbing the severe banks just as well as the Drummonds in the race of 1895 but with *double the loads*. The design was developed through four successive enlargements, known as the 'Dunalastair II', 'III' and 'IV' series, and finally there were the superheated developments of the Type IV. The 'Dunalastair II' series achieved an international reputation, because the design was accepted without any alteration for service on the Belgian National Railways.

69 A Highland 'Loch'; one of David Jones's 4-4-os.

In his earlier 4-4-0 locomotives for the Highland Railway Jones had perpetuated the massive double framing at the front end, with the outside cylinders snugly ensconced between the two parts of the framing, and very rigidly secured thereby. This was a legacy from the practice of Alexander Allan, introduced at a time when locomotive construction had scarcely emerged from its infancy and there was difficulty sometimes in maintaining the cylinder fastening secure. In 1896, when the majority of British engines still favoured inside cylinders, Jones retained them outside, but with greatly improved constructional methods abandoned the double framing on the 'Lochs', and produced an extremely simple locomotive thereby. The 'Lochs' were in the very top flight among passenger engines of the day. Massively built, skilfully designed, and economical to run, they quickly became great favourites with their drivers. This, Jones's successor in office learned some years later. On a very special occasion the new engineer intended to run an express from Perth to Inverness with two of his own engines. The men demanded that on such an auspicious occasion they must have two Jones 4-4-os; the newer ones were not *suitable*! Many years later, during World War I, when additional engines were needed for the Dingwall and Skye line for the wartime traffic, three more 'Lochs' were built, exactly to the original drawings of 1896. One could not wish for a finer tribute to an excellent design.

70 Great North of Scotland Railway; engines of this handsome design introduced in 1899.

Following the resignation of W. Cowan, the G.N.S.R. was served successively by two engineers who later moved to much larger Scottish Railways: James Manson, who went to the Glasgow and South Western, and W. Pickersgill, who went to the Caledonian. In 1899 Pickersgill designed a particularly handsome 4-4-0, and ten were ordered from Neilson and Co. of Glasgow. When the time came for delivery, traffic on the G.N.S.R. had declined to such an extent that the Company could not afford them, and five were purchased by the English South Eastern and Chatham Railway. But the five taken by the G.N.S.R. became the first of the final development of motive power on the railway, and eight further engines of the class were built at Inverurie Works between 1909 and 1915. After World War I when T. E. Heywood had succeeded Pickersgill as Locomotive Superintendent, eight new 4-4-os were added to the stock, similar to Pickersgill's 1899 class, but having superheaters. The eight engines of the new superheater class were all named, and it is one of these, the *Gordon Highlander*, that has been preserved. In Heywood's time the picturesque green livery of the locomotives was superseded by black, and in G.N.S.R. days the *Gordon Highlander* never carried the original green. When the engine was withdrawn for preservation and restored, it was painted in the green livery, as shown in our picture.

71 Webb 4-cylinder Compound; L.&N.W.R.

After building a large number of three-cylinder compounds, with the curious arrangement of having two small high pressure cylinders, and one huge low pressure cylinder, Webb turned to four-cylinder compounds. His 4-4-0 passenger engines with this arrangement were largely a failure, but in applying the principle to a heavy mineral engine Webb produced about the best and longest-lived compounds of his career. The valve layout that made his passenger compounds so sluggish was no handicap in a hard-slogging slow-moving coal engine, and these massive though rather ungainly engines did many years of excellent work. Out of the 170 built between 1901 and 1940 60 of them still remained as compounds in 1923. Others were converted into two-cylinder simple engines. But one of the interesting developments concerned the wheel arrangement. A mere glance at our picture is enough to suggest that there was considerable weight overhanging at the front end. All four cylinders were in line, and with some of the engines trouble was experienced from this overhanging weight. Webb's successor, George Whale, rebuilt a number of these engines by inserting a pony truck at the leading end, thus converting them from 0-8-0 to 2-8-0.

Some of the engines thus rebuilt were fitted with much larger boilers, and these latter engines formed the virtual prototype for the celebrated 'Super D' o-8-os of later years.

72 **The First British 'Atlantic';** Great Northern.

The death of Patrick Stirling in November 1895, was followed by the appointment of H. A. Ivatt, from the Great Southern and Western Railway, of Ireland. Ivatt had, however, been trained at Crewe, and although in size and power his locomotives for the Great Northern came eventually to look very different from those of Stirling it was nevertheless a process of development rather than a metamorphosis. Within two years of taking office Ivatt had produced a huge engine, No. 990, the first British locomotive of the Atlantic type, though in so doing he beat Mr Aspinall of the Lancashire and Yorkshire Railway for the honour by no more than a matter of months. The first Ivatt 'Atlantics' appeared in the same year as the memorable 'Gold Rush' and were nicknamed the 'Klondykes' in consequence. They were handsomely proportioned, and immediately displayed a haulage capacity far above that of the Stirling 'singles'. The pioneer engine, No. 990, was named *Henry Oakley*, after the General Manager of the company, and a further 20 engines were built later. They did excellent work on the line, though in 1902 Ivatt to some extent superseded his own creation by producing a modified version with a greatly enlarged boiler. As the pioneer of the Atlantic type in Great Britain, of course, the *Henry Oakley* is a most historic engine, and it is preserved in the Railway Museum at York.

73 **The First British 4-6-0;** Highland Railway.

From the moment he was authorized to build new locomotives David Jones put the Highland Railway in the forefront of British locomotive practice; and from the honour of possessing in 1874 one of the heaviest and most powerful locomotives in Europe, Jones created something of a sensation 20 years later when he built the first British examples of the 4-6-0 type. In designing something very much larger than anything that had gone before, it might well have been thought that Jones was venturing into the unknown, and would have proceeded cautiously, with a single prototype – or two at the outside. On the contrary an order was placed with Sharp Stewart and Co. for 15 of these huge engines, straight off the drawing board. Moreover they proved absolutely 'right' from the very beginning. There were no teething troubles. To use motor-car parlance, the men 'stepped in and drove away'. Although primarily intended for goods traffic they were free-running engines, and were used on passenger trains during the heavy traffic of the tourist season. It is believed that some of them, when new, were painted in the Stroudley style of old, with 'Brighton yellow' as the basic colour; but in our picture we have shown one of these engines in the standard Jones style, with a basis of apple green. Engine No. 109 of this class has been restored to a reproduction of the original condition, and has done a great deal of interesting work in Scotland in the haulage of special trains.

74 **The Aspinall Atlantic;** Lancashire and Yorkshire Railway.

It was a race between the Great Northern and the Lancashire and Yorkshire Railway as to which would produce the first Atlantic engine to run in Great Britain. The Great Northern won the race, but the Lancashire produced an engine of great character and distinction. In some ways the 'Highflyers', so called because of the high pitch of their boilers, could be described as an enlarged and elongated version of Aspinall's 4-4-0 of 1891. But the

'Atlantics' were notable in having a very large boiler, and a Belpaire firebox, both of which features placed them far apart from the 4-4-os. They were designed for high speed running over all parts of the system with heavier trains than could be taken by the 4-4-os. When they first appeared in 1899, locomotive enthusiasts and railwaymen alike were positively staggered by the size of these 'Atlantics', and their running, particularly on the Liverpool and Manchester service, was at times breathtaking, not only in the maximum speeds attained but in their acceleration from rest. With them it was nothing to pass Salford, a mere ¾ mile out of Manchester, at over 50 m.p.h. On a trial run from Liverpool to Southport, in 1899, with a 5-coach train, one of them is reported to have attained a speed of almost 100 m.p.h. All 40 of them passed into L.M.S.R. ownership, and the last of them was not scrapped until October 1933.

75 Taff Vale Railway; One of T. Hurry Riches' o-6-o tank engines.

The Taff Vale was an amazing railway. Its main line ran from Cardiff to Ponty-pridd, and there forked – one line going up the Rhondda Valley and the other to Merthyr. At its greatest extent it had a route mileage of little more than 110, and yet it owned, in 1922, no fewer than 271 locomotives. At the zenith of the coal export boom its trains positively queued up at the entrance to the Cardiff Docks, but amid the teeming coal traffic the company managed to run a swarm of local passenger trains. As on the other railways in South Wales, the o-6-2 tank was a very popular type. It was equally handy for goods and pasenger working, and the fashion for this type in South Wales can well have been set by the fine engine illustrated in our picture. Eventually the Taff Vale had no fewer than 150 locomotives of this wheel arrangement. Riches was locomotive superintendent of

the railway from 1873 to 1910, and it was indeed a measure of his stature in the engineering world that he was elected President of the Institution of Mechanical Engineers in 1906–7, a very high honour for a man from so relatively small a railway. Our picture cannot show in any detail the striking coat of arms of the Taff Vale Railway, which includes a positively riotous example of the Red Dragon of Wales

76 Barry Railway; handsome passenger tank engine.

It is perhaps inappropriate to have, as representative of one of the South Wales 'coal' railways, a locomotive used exclusively in passenger service. But the passenger activities of the Barry Railway were so typical of the unbounded enterprise of the company, and the o-4-4 tank engines were so brilliantly turned out that they have been chosen in preference to the less ornate, work-horse engines that handled the coal trains. The Barry Railway owned its origin to the congestion of traffic on the Taff Vale and Rhymney lines, and was built primarily to carry coal. And from its opening in 1888 it did this in great quantities. But having started on the way to establishing a new town at Barry Island a passenger service was inaugurated, and soon became an important item in the company's activities. The Barry Railway was indeed the only one of the local South Wales to participate in the running of a main line service – the celebrated 'Ports to Ports Express', between Barry and Newcastle-upon-Tyne. This service was operated in conjunction with such giants of the railway world as the Great Western, the Great Central, and the North Eastern. The Barry locomotives hauled this express between Cardiff and Barry, and the smart little o-4-4 tanks were used for this duty. They were certainly not the least handsome of the locomotives that hauled that express on its long journey.

77 **Rhymney Railway;** a mixed traffic tank engine.

The Rhymney Railway was a purely local concern in South Wales, a child of the prodigious boom in the coal trade during the Victorian Era. It began at the head of the Rhymney river valley, among high mountains, and it ended at the Cardiff docks. The coal it conveyed for export reached at times to astronomical quantities, but there was also a thriving passenger business between such centres of population as Caerphilly Ystrad Mynach, Bargoed, and Rhymney. The locomotives therefore had all to be general purpose machines, and the engine illustrated is typical of the workmanlike 0-6-2 tank designs introduced from 1906 onwards by Mr C. T. Hurry Riches. This able engineer was a son of the famous locomotive superintendent of the neighbouring Taff Vale Railway. The new superintendent of the Rhymney Railway came to Caerphilly Works from the Great Central Railway, and in the Welsh valleys he imparted much of the grace and smart turnout of Gorton to the goods and passenger engines of the Rhymney. Both classes of engine carried the green livery, lined out, and having chocolate brown underframes, while the engines particularly allocated to passenger working had polished brass domes, and brass pedestals for the safety valves. Unlike its neighbour, the Brecon and Merthyr, the Rhymney Railway used the Westinghouse brake.

78 **Brecon and Merthyr Railway;** mineral tank engine.

This railway, despite its name, does not actually enter Merthyr on its own metals, but it provides a long and important link in the chain of communication between the mining valleys of South Wales and the fine farming country north of the Brecknock Beacons. There are some extremely heavy gradients on the way, particularly in the long descent from Torpantau Tunnel to Talybont-on-Usk, where the gradient is 1 in 38 for many miles. A humorist once declared, indeed, that the Brecon and Merthyr Railway would do well as a toboggan run! These fine engines, built by Robert Stephenson and Company to the design of James Dunbar, had 4 ft. 6 in. coupled wheels – ideal for the heavy grades – yet even these engines were limited to a maximum load of 10 loaded wagons and a brake van up the 1 in 38 gradients. It can be well imagined how much double-heading was necessary with the freight trains before the introduction of these powerful locomotives. They were not confined to freight. At one time there was a brisk passenger business over this route, with through carriages from Cardiff (Taff Vale line) via Merthyr to Brecon and the seaside resorts on Cardigan Bay. This was additional to the regular passenger service from Newport via Bargoed. These engines were equipped with the automatic vacuum brake so that they could assist in the passenger traffic.

79 **London Brighton and South Coast Railway;** 'B4' class.

When Billinton succeeded to the office of Locomotive Superintendent of the L.B.&S.C.R. in 1889, after the death of Stroudley, he at once abandoned the principle of front-coupled express locomotives, and in his first design, the 'B2' class of 1895, he used the conventional 4-4-0 wheel arrangement. This first class, nicknamed the 'Grasshoppers', were not successful. The boiler was too small, and on the Portsmouth line the new engines did very little better than the old Stroudley 'singles' of 1880. But in his second 4-4-0 design, the 'B4' class of 1901, Billinton made no mistake. They were splendid engines in every way, and had no difficulty in running the 51 miles between Victoria and Brighton in the hour – sometimes considerably less. When they were newly built they carried the beautiful Stroudley livery, with all its gay colouring in addition to the famous 'yellow'. But they were best known in the handsome chocolate brown of later Brighton days, set off with much black and yellow lining out. Engine No. 70 was originally named *Holyrood*, and she made a record run from Victoria to Brighton with the Sunday Pullman train on July 26, 1903: 51 miles in 48¾ min. start to stop. In later years, when she was carrying the chocolate livery, the engine was named *Devonshire*, as illustrated. The 'B4' class went generally by the name of the 'Scotchmen', because most of them were built in Glasgow, by Sharp, Stewart and Co. Ltd.

80 An Oil-Fired 4-2-2, of 1898; Great Eastern Railway.

The last single-driver express locomotive built for the Great Eastern was designed specially for the accelerated Cromer expresses of 1896. Until then, passengers for that rising resort of the Norfolk coast had to change at Norwich. At first the new Cromer expresses stopped at Ipswich, but later the run was made non-stop. In the season the loads were particularly heavy, including a dining car and some bogie corridor vehicles. But not many of the latter had then been built, and a typical load of one of these Cromer expresses would be 12 six-wheelers, 4 bogie coaches, and a 4-wheeled fruit van. To handle these long and heavy trains, at an average speed of 49 m.p.h. throughout, James Holden built ten of the very handsome 4-2-2 locomotives illustrated. On their first introduction these trains had been worked by the '1000' class 2-2-2s, but the big 4-2-2s took over in the summer of 1898. Four of the latter were stationed at Ipswich, and four at Norwich. The London–Cromer non-stops were all worked as lodging turns, by Ipswich and Norwich men on alternate days. The Ipswich engines started at their home shed, worked to London, and then took the Cromer non-stop. Then they worked back to Norwich and lodged. On the following day they did the trip in reverse. In their later years they followed their predecessors to the Joint Line, and finished a short but brilliant career running the York expresses of the Great Eastern Railway.

81 Great Central Railway; a Pollitt 4-4-0.

In 1893 the Manchester, Sheffield and Lincolnshire Railway obtained its Act authorizing the extension to London, and in 1897 the title of the railway was changed to Great Central. In readiness for the London express services Harry Pollitt designed a class of 4-4-0. These engines proved very successful, but in later years the new locomotive superintendent, J. G. Robinson, greatly improved them by adding superheaters, and a commodious canopied cab. These engines were soon displaced by larger machines on the London Extension but they then became the mainstay of the Cheshire Lines passenger services. In rapid acceleration, and fast running between stops they earned such a reputation for reliability that the Liverpool and Manchester trains became known as the 'Punctual' expresses. On this duty the rebuilt Pollitt 4-4-0s were in competition with very fast rival services on *two* other routes between Liverpool and Manchester namely those of the London and North Western, and of the Lancashire and Yorkshire. All three routes provided a 40-minute service between the two cities, though on the Cheshire Lines in some ways the hardest work was involved on those trains making an intermediate stop at Warrington, and completing the 34 miles from Manchester to Liverpool in 45 minutes, inclusive of the stop.

82 North Eastern Railway; One of the 'R' class 4-4-0s.

The turn of the century on the railways

of Great Britain was a time of greatly increased train loads, and of a growing realization that operation must be more economically performed. Following the great success of the 'M' class engines, by the standards of the nineteenth century, Wilson Worsdell set out to design an enlarged version that should be capable of taking much heavier loads, but which would also be capable of a much longer day's work. It was still a time for each driver to have his own engine, but in the 'R' class each engine had two regular crews, who worked in two shifts. The 'R' class were not only excellent engines in hard weight pulling, but they proved capable of doing practically double the daily mileage previously considered normal for an express locomotive. They were immensely popular with their crews, and so far as the double-manning was concerned, a typical day's work would go from Newcastle to Edinburgh and back with the first crew, and then from Newcastle to Leeds and back with the second. Among other duties they ran what was then the fastest start-to-stop run in the country: 1.9 p.m. Darlington to York, 44.1 miles in 43 min. The trip was frequently done at much higher speeds, and a record was made by engine No. 1672, when the start-to-stop time was 39½ min. Some of these engines lasted for more than 50 years.

83 **Furness Railway;** Pettigrew 4-4-0. Although no more than a local railway, the Furness was held in unusually high esteem, partly because of the great importance of its traffic, and still more so because of the status of its Locomotive Engineer. Pettigrew was associated with William Adams of the London and South Western Railway in some of the most important and comprehensive tests carried out on British locomotives in the nineteenth century. He was also the author of the standard work on locomotive constructional practice at the time. One looks with particular interest, therefore, to the locomotives he designed for the Furness Railway, and one is not disappointed. The handsome and powerful 4-4-os, of which an example forms the subject of our picture, could be described as an inside cylinder version of the famous Adams 4-4-0 of the L.&S.W.R. While the Furness line did not give an opportunity for sustained fast running there were certainly some very smartly timed trains, particularly the early morning mail, booked to run the 19 miles from Carnforth to Ulverston in 24 min. Although level, the line makes a winding course, very close to the sea, and to keep such a schedule involved very rapid acceleration, and a steady 60 m.p.h. thereafter. These 4-4-os also did well on the heavy gradients experienced in crossing the Barrow isthmus. An attractive feature of all Furness locomotives was the pleasing shade of red that was the basis of their livery – 'iron-ore red' – very appropriate to the district in which they worked.

84 **Cambrian Railways;** a passenger 4-4-0.
The Cambrian Railways – always in the plural – was a difficult system to manage, with its main line running from Whitchurch up the Severn Valley, and then through mountainous country to the sea at Aberystwyth, and some very long and meandering branches. Furthermore, its administrative headquarters and locomotive works was clean outside Wales, at Oswestry, in Shropshire. From Dovey Junction a line made its way right round the northern arc of Cardigan Bay to Pwllheli, while from Moat Lane Junction another line followed a chain of valleys in Central Wales, to Brecon. And yet, for all its far flung extent the Cambrian had much more of a main line character than the busy local railways of South Wales. Its trains savoured of long-time, if not long-distance travel, and this was re-

flected in the locomotive power employed. Very few tank engines were used, and on the main line trains a change was made from the 2-4-0 to the 4-4-0 type of tender engine in 1878. The engine shown in our picture is of a later and much larger class, designed by Mr Aston and first built by Sharp, Stewart and Company in 1893. They were excellent machines, and for many years hauled the main line trains, carrying through carriages from Aberystwyth to Manchester, Birmingham and London. The Cambrian engines, although painted black, had the distinction of carrying the insignia of the Prince of Wales on their tenders.

85 Somerset and Dorset Joint Railway; a 4-4-0 of 1903.

The Somerset and Dorset was a joint concern of the London and South Western, and the Midland Railway. Its main line ran from Bath to Bournemouth, and it involved some exceedingly heavy gradients in the crossing of the Mendips. Because of the joint ownership engineering responsibility for the working of the line was divided; the L.&S.W.R. maintained the track and the signalling, while the Midland had the responsibility for locomotives. Between Bath and Evercreech Junction the ruling gradient is 1 in 50, and for the S.&D. working it was considered desirable to modify the standard Midland express engines by providing them with smaller wheels to cope with the inclines involved in crossing the Mendips. The engine chosen for illustration is, however, particularly interesting. Instead of being an adaptation of a Midland design to suit S.&D. conditions it was virtually a new Derby design, of which a subsequent adaptation with *larger* coupled wheels became a Midland Railway standard. It was the first time Derby had used this particular type of boiler on a 4-4-0 locomotive. The coupled wheels were 6 ft. in diameter, and when subsequently it was decided to rebuild a number of the older Midland 4-4-0 locomotives with larger boilers, this S.&D. boiler was applied to engines with 6 ft. 6 in. coupled wheels.

86 Midland and Great Northern Joint Railway; an express passenger 4-4-0.

This interesting joint line, now completely closed and dismantled, at one time carried a considerable traffic from the East Midlands to East Anglia. It was an amalgamation of a number of smaller local railways, and was jointly owned, as its name implied, by the Midland and the Great Northern Railways. Some of the locomotives were precisely of standard Midland design, though instantly distinguished by the handsome mustard-yellow livery. The locomotive works of the Joint Line were at Melton Constable, and there, under the supervision of William Marriott, Locomotive Superintendent, the locomotives we illustrate were rebuilt from a Midland design of 1894. At the same time the rebuilding made use of many parts that were standard Derby fittings at the time, such as the chimney tapering outwards from the base, the safety cover, and the canopied cab. The curious thing is, however, that these features never appeared simultaneously on a contemporary Midland engine. The M.&G.N. main line from Norwich to its point of junction with the Midland Railway near Saxby, includes much heavy grading, and these engines worked through between Norwich and Leicester, each engine and crew working the fast expresses on alternate days, and lodging at Leicester overnight.

87 Lynton and Barnstaple narrow gauge railway; one of the tank engines.

The Lynton and Barnstaple was one of the unluckiest of light railways. It was built to provide rail communication of a kind, to the remote twin towns of Lynton and Lynmouth, approached by only rough and indifferent roads. The line to Barnstaple was opened in 1898, but there had been much miscalculation in the estimates and the line cost far more than had been allowed for. Once opened, it proved a very popular line for summer visitors; but it never really paid its way, and for some years after grouping the Southern Railway lavished money upon some publicity, but still operated it at a loss. Eventually in the autumn of 1935 it was closed. This sad event was long before the days of amateur preservation societies for these picturesque little railways. It would have formed an unrivalled object for such attention had closure been threatened some ten or a dozen years later. The 2-6-2 tank engines were built specially for the line by Manning, Wardle and Co. of Leeds. The first three were delivered for the opening of the line, and were happily named after 3-letter Devon rivers *Yeo*, *Exe* and *Taw*. Another engine of the same type, *Lew*, was added after the Southern Railway had assumed responsibility in 1923. They were then painted in standard livery, with the name SOUTHERN extending from end to end of the side tanks.

88 Leek and Manifold Light Railway; one of the tank engines.

Towards the end of the Victorian era the policy was formed of constructing cheaply-built light railways in rural districts to act as feeders to the main line systems, in areas where the prospective traffic did not warrant the building of ordinary branch lines. Certain relaxations from the ordinary Board of Trade requirements were permitted as a result of an Act of Parliament dated 1896, and great hopes for success were expressed as a result of this legislation. The Leek and Manifold Light Railway was built under the provisions of this Act, amid the beautiful hills and dales of the south-western corner of the Derbyshire Peak District. It was opened in 1904, and worked by two picturesque 2-6-4 tank engines. Our picture shows one of these in the handsome chocolate livery originally used. Later the North Staffordshire Railway livery was adopted, and when the latter company came within the L.M.S. group the two little Manifold tank engines were painted in Midland red. Unhappily the railway never paid. After World War I local buses provided a much more convenient service, though the railway was kept going, at a considerable loss, until 1934. One notable feature of the locomotives was their huge headlight, needed because much of the line was unfenced, and unprotected by gates at level crossings.

89 Festiniog Railway; one of the 'double-engines'.

The Festiniog Railway was built to convey slates from the quarries of Blaenau Festiniog to Portmadoc for shipment, and while heavy loaded trains could be worked down the valley without difficulty there was congestion on the line because of the limited loads of empties that could be hauled up the steep gradients from the coast. Robert Fairlie then devised the famous double-engine, consisting of two engine units, back to back, with two boilers fed from a central double firebox. Although the double boiler is built as a single unit structurally, there are actually separate fireboxes and separate firedoors. The water and steam space is continuous throughout. The first 'double engine', the *Little Wonder* showed its ability to haul more than twice the load of any engine already on the line, and after 1869 a number of double engines were put to work. Two of them still survive today, and after lying derelict in the Boston Lodge Works for very many years both have been restored to first-class working order, and are giving excellent service on the railway today. The Fairlie articulated engines of the Festiniog

Railway represent a most historic development in steam locomotives. The principle of articulation, so putting what is virtually an assembly of two engines under the control of a single crew, was developed strikingly in the Beyer-Garratt type of locomotive, to which reference is made later.

90 Snowdon Mountain Railway; one of the Swiss-built rack locomotives.

Tremendous interest was created when the Snowdon Mountain Tramroad and Hotels Co. Ltd. – to give the concern its original title – was incorporated in November 1894. The line climbs from Llanberis to the summit of Snowdon, 3500 ft. above sea level, in 5 miles, with a maximum steepness of ascent of 1 in 6. The gauge is 2 ft. $7\frac{1}{2}$ in. and there is a double steel rack for engaging the locomotive pinions. The locomotive *Wyddfa* is one of three supplied by the Swiss Locomotive Company of Winterthur, for the opening of the line, in 1895; but of that trio, one was destroyed in a sensational accident, in which the locomotive left the rails on a high, exposed ridge, and plunged thousands of feet to destruction. Following that, additional safety devices were included, and the line has been operated with complete safety since its opening to regular traffic in April 1897. There are seven locomotives in service, all of the 0-4-2 type, but varying in detail. In addition to the two survivors of the original trio, both of which are still doing good work, there are two dating from 1896, and three newer ones supplied from Switzerland in 1922–3. Each 'train' consists of one coach, seating 60 passengers, and on the upward journey it is propelled by the locomotive. By reason of the exceptional steepness of the ascent, and the need for the utmost caution when descending the mountain, speed is limited in both directions to a maximum of 5 m.p.h.

91 The 'Claud Hamilton'; epoch-making Great Eastern 4-4-0.

For upwards of 40 years successive locomotive superintendents of the Great Eastern Railway had built little save single-driver express locomotives. Where there had been coupled engines, as with the otherwise identical '1000' class 2-2-2, and 'T.19' 2-4-0 of James Holden, the singles had proved as good as, if not better than, the coupled engines. But by the turn of the century something considerably larger was needed. The crack expresses were being equipped with corridor coaches throughout, and restaurant cars, and the loads of the holiday trains were rising from 250 to 350 tons. Under James Holden's supervision the *Claud Hamilton* engine was designed and built at Stratford, in 1900. It was much larger and more powerful than anything previously seen on the G.E.R., and where the 'singles' had tackled trains up to 250 tons in weight, the 'Claud Hamilton' class 4-4-0s could, when really extended, take *four hundred* tons. Again, while most of the 'singles' had a very short life some of the 'Claud Hamiltons', through various processes of rebuilding, lasted for more than fifty years. The first engine, No. 1900, was the only one to be named, after Lord Claud Hamilton, the Chairman of the Great Eastern Railway. The original design had a boiler with a round-topped firebox, but later varieties were fitted with Belpaire types. They rank among the most successful 4-4-0 express passenger locomotives ever built.

92 A Johnson 'Belpaire'; Midland Railway.

Throughout the nineteenth century the Midland had been a railway with locomotives of slender proportions and exceedingly graceful appearance, and a study of the examples shown under our references 47, 60 and 66 makes it clear that they had a strongly characteristic style of their own. At the turn of the century train loads were very much on the increase; the stimulus of competition demanded accelerated service, and these demands were reflected in a profound change in the traditional appearance of Midland locomotives. The large-boilered 4-4-os built at Derby at the turn of the century had the square-topped Belpaire fireboxes, and large bogie tenders, to enable them to make long non-stop runs with heavy trains. As the first engines on the Midland to have this particular type of firebox they were always known as the 'Belpaires', even in later years when there were many locomotives of other types running with Belpaire fireboxes. When the Midland decided to instal water troughs the large bogie tenders became unnecessary, and these engines were fitted with a standard six-wheeled non-bogie type. In later years they were renumbered in the '700' series, and their usefulness was further increased in the nineteen-twenties when they were fitted with superheaters.

93 Hull and Barnsley Railway; Matthew Stirling's express locomotive.

The Hull and Barnsley Railway was built as an alternative, highly competitive route for conveying coal from the South Yorkshire coalfield to Hull, for export to Scandinavia and the Baltic states. At the same time this enterprising line attempted to build up a fast passenger service between Hull and Sheffield. From 1885, until the railway was absorbed into the L.N.E.R. group, the locomotive superintendent was Matthew Stirling, son of the celebrated Patrick Stirling of the Great Northern, and nephew of James Stirling. Like his father and his uncle, Matthew Stirling was firmly attached to locomotives with domeless boilers. His freight engines were 0-6-os and 0-8-os, but until the year 1910 he had not found it necessary to build anything larger than 2-4-os for passenger traffic. Then, however, he introduced the handsome 4-4-0 design

shown in our picture. Though not so richly endowed with flowing curves and nineteenth-century elegance as one of his father's engines, this 4-4-0, of which design five were eventually in service, represents a worthy development of the Stirling tradition in locomotive constructional practice. They did admirable work on the Sheffield–Hull expresses, from 1910 until the re-arrangement of the train services some time after grouping, in 1923.

94 The 'City of Truro'; Great Western Railway.

These locomotives, although relatively few in number, gained great fame for their designer, for the G.W.R., and for British railways in general. Technically they represent an important link in the chain of development of locomotive practice at Swindon, from the Victorian traditions of the Dean period to twentieth-century standards. They retained the outside frames of former days, and cylinders with slide valves, but they incorporated the very important advance of the tapered-barrel boiler, and Belpaire firebox. In high-speed express traffic with trains of moderate weight they were outstandingly successful, improving upon the new standards of running set by immediate predecessors of the 'Atbara' class, which were similar, but with parallel boilers. Engine No. 3433 *City of Bath* set up a new record for the London–Plymouth run made non-stop, via Bristol, in $233\frac{1}{2}$ min. for the distance of 246.6 miles; this record was made with an advance portion of the Cornishman express in 1903. Engine No. 3440 *City of Truro* reached a maximum speed of slightly over 100 m.p.h. near Wellington, with an Ocean Mail special in May 1904. In ordinary service these engines were responsible for the first regular running of the Cornish Riviera Express non-stop in each direction between Paddington and Plymouth 245.6 miles in 267 min.

The *City of Truro* has been preserved, and is now in the Great Western Railway Museum at Swindon.

95 A 'Precursor' Class 4-4-0; London and North Western Railway.

Webb's large scale experiment with compound locomotives had left the L.N.W.R. short of powerful and reliable engines, and the first task of his successor, George Whale, was to provide for that deficiency. Under his direction a simple, straightforward 4-4-0 was designed in record time at Crewe Works; in some ways it was a much larger version of the 'Precedent' class 2-4-0, but with the important difference of having Joy valve gear instead of the Allan straight-link motion. Within 10 months from the time of Webb's retirement the first engine of the new class, No. 513 *Precursor* was on the road, and it proved an immediate and outstanding success. There were no teething troubles, and after a first batch of ten, constructed at intervals between March and June 1904, quantity production began in earnest, and a level 100 of them were completed at Crewe between October 1904 and May 1906. At times they were turning them out at the rate of 2 per week! And what engines they were. They proved an absolute godsend to the Running Department, by their almost unfailing reliability, taking loads of 350 to 400 tons on schedules demanding average speeds of 52 to 55 m.p.h. from start to stop. Twenty more of them were constructed in 1907. The engine illustrated, No. 1111 *Cerberus*, was the first of eight engines of the class completed at Crewe in the one month of March 1905, when production of them was at its height.

96 Earle-Marsh's 'I3' Tank; London Brighton and South Coast Railway.

Basically these engines, introduced by D. Earle-Marsh in 1907, could be des-cribed as a tank engine version of the Billinton 'B4' express passenger 4-4-0 (reference 79). The 'I3' class were express locomotives in every way, with 6 ft. 6 in. coupled wheels, and for the relatively short runs of the Brighton railway they were handier and more compact than a tender engine at the terminals. But when Marsh equipped some of these engines with the Schmidt superheater he trans-formed them into one of the most economical locomotive classes ever to run south of the Thames. In 1909 one of them, No. 23, was engaged in comparative trials on the 'Sunny South Special' express service, as between Rugby and Brighton. The competing engine was a L.N.W.R. non-superheated 'Precursor' type 4-4-0, and although the circumstances for the two engines were not necessarily identical the Brighton engine showed a remarkable economy in both coal and water con-sumption, while running the trains with conspicuous ease. It is generally con-sidered that the working of the 4-4-2 tank engine No. 23 influenced the decision of the L.N.W.R. to introduce superheating on a considerable scale. The Brighton tank engines had a long and arduous life, and some of them were still doing excellent work on the non-electrified sections of the Southern Railway as recently as 1947. The last survivor was scrapped in 1953.

97 The De Glehn 4-4-2 'La France'; Great Western Railway.

At the turn of the century much attention was focussed upon current French loco-motive practice by the very successful running of the various classes of four-cylinder compound on the Northern Railway. These engines were designed upon the system of Mr Alfred de Glehn, an English engineer, who was then Chief Engineer of the Société Alsacienne of Belfort. The introduction of the Nord compound Atlantics made some quite spectacular accelerations of the English boat trains possible, as between Paris and

Calais, and many English engineers gave consideration anew to the use of the compound system. On the Great Western Churchward arranged for a French-built compound 'Atlantic' to be purchased, and the *La France*, delivered in 1903, ran a series of trials on the principal Great Western expresses in competition with Swindon-built engines. For the most part these were not 'set' trials, but they involved the careful observation, month in, month out, of general performance, reliability, running costs, fuel consumption and so on. While these did not show any superiority over the Swindon-built ten-wheelers *La France*, and the two larger French compounds purchased in 1905, included some features of detail design that became standard practice on the G.W.R., notably the bogie, and design of big-end for the inside cylinder connecting rods. The principal feature that was copied, however, was the division of the drive between two axles – the inside cylinders driving on to the leading pair of coupled wheels.

98 Dugald Drummond's 'T9'; London and South Western Railway.

This class, of which 66 were built between the years 1899 and 1901, represented the culmination of Dugald Drummond's 'small' 4-4-0 design, which was initiated on the North British Railway in 1876, and developed on the Caledonian and brought to its final and most successful form on the London and South Western. A smaller-wheeled variant of the same design was put into service on the Highland Railway by Peter Drummond. The engine illustrated, No. 714, belongs to the second batch of 1899, which had cross-water tubes in the firebox, designed to promote more rapid circulation of the water, and quicker steam raising. The cover over the ends of these tubes is seen between the coupled wheel splashers. Although slender in appearance these engines were capable of very hard work on the road. The

coupled wheelbase (10ft.) was exceptionally long, and permitted of a large firebox grate area. In consequence the capacity for steam raising was good, and enabled the engines to haul heavy trains and do work that belied their slender appearance. They could run very fast, and on the Salisbury-Exeter road frequently attained speeds of 85 m.p.h. and over. In later years a number of them were rebuilt with extended smokeboxes, superheaters, and stove-pipe chimneys, and one of these latter has been preserved, and is painted in L.&S.W.R. colours.

99 Lancashire and Yorkshire Railways; one of the side tank engines.

In addition to its many and various main lines the Lancashire and Yorkshire had numerous branches, some extending into very hilly country on the Lancashire side of the Pennines. Aspinall introduced the 2-4-2 side tank type of locomotive in 1899, indeed engine No. 1008 was not only the first of the class, but also the first engine to be built new at Horwich Works. No fewer than 210 of the original type were built, down to the year 1898; but after that, the type was developed to the very efficient superheater version of 1911. Our picture shows an engine of 1905 vintage, originally built to use saturated steam, but modernized by the addition of a superheater in 1921. In this, their final form, they were remarkable little engines, pulling heavy loads on the longer-distance residential trains from Manchester. One of the hardest runs was an evening non-stop from Salford to Colne, on which the usual load was one of 10 non-corridor carriages, filled almost entirely with first-class season ticket holders. In climbing into the hills there is a stretch where the gradient averages 1 in 118 for 15 miles, and these little tank engines used to run that heavy train with the punctuality of chronometers. Altogether the Lancashire and Yorkshire Railway owned 330 of these 2-4-2 tank engines. Many of them put in more than 50 years of service, and some lasted for over 60 years.

100 **London and South Western Railway;** the 'M7' tank engine.
This class, of which no fewer than 105 were built between 1897 and 1911, can be considered among Dugald Drummond's 'small' engine designs. They represent the only example on the L.&S.W.R. of an affinity, so far as wheel arrangement was concerned, to Stroudley's front-coupled types on the Brighton railway. They were splendid engines in every way, and many of them have put in more than 60 years of service. They originally ran the London suburban trains, and locals on many country branches. Although their coupled wheels were only 5 ft. 7 in. diameter as against 6 ft. 7 in. on the express passenger engines they could run very freely, and were used on the longer-distance residential trains from Waterloo in addition to purely suburban services. Beautifully constructed, they were veritable little 'Rolls Royces' among tank engines, and rode with a quietness, ease, and silence that would have been the envy of many a driver on a far more spectacular main line passenger engine. In their later days they were still very familiar sights at Waterloo, working trains of empty coaches between the carriage sidings at Clapham and the terminus.

101 **Stroudley's 'D' Class 0-4-2 Tank.**
This was another very successful Stroudley design, used in heavy suburban and branch line passenger service all over the Brighton system. The first of them was built in 1873, and it was undoubtedly the favourable experience gained with these engines in semi-fast traffic that led Mr Stroudley towards the use of front coupled driving wheels in the 'Gladstone' class. There were no fewer than 125 of the 'D' class, built between the years 1873 and 1887, and all of them were named after stations on the line. It must be admitted that this system of naming was applied both to these engines and to the smaller 'A' class with the 0-6-0 wheel arrangement in a somewhat unimaginative way. One feels also that those concerned either had their tongues in their cheeks, or were devoid of a sense of humour – otherwise one of these splendid little engines would never have been named *Crawley*! They were strongly built, almost unfailingly reliable, and in consequence long-lived. After the L.B.& S.C.R. became part of the Southern Railway many of the 'D' class were drafted to country branches far from the old Brighton line, and some of them reached the ripe old age of 70 years before they were finally withdrawn from service. Originally they were painted in the Stroudley yellow livery.

102 **Great Eastern Railway;** the London suburban tank engine of 1890–1902.
At the time of the grouping, in 1923, the Great Eastern Railway was operating, entirely by steam, the heaviest suburban traffic in London. The development of the outer residential districts coupled with the increase in local traffic had placed a tremendous strain upon the traffic-handling capacity of Liverpool Street Station, and the Operating Superintendent, F. V. Russell, remodelled the entire timetables, in addition to making a large number of small but significant alterations to the track layout, so as to run many more trains in the rush hours. To cut down the time spent at intermediate stations the carriage doors were painted different colours to denote the three classes, so that passengers could quickly recognize the whereabouts of the class they wanted. These services became known as the 'Jazz trains', in consequence of the coloured doors. They were worked by small, but very sturdy and reliable 0-6-0 tank engines, having small wheels

for rapid acceleration from many stops. From Liverpool Street they worked the 'Jazz' service to Enfield, Palace Gates, Walthamstow and Chingford, and did remarkable work for many years. The design was originally introduced in 1890 by James Holden, though an improved version, with higher boiler pressure and larger side tanks, dates from 1902. No fewer than 134 of them were still in service on the nationalized British Railways in 1949.

103 'Cardean' of the Caledonian.

It is doubtful if any single locomotive built in the first decade of the twentieth century achieved, at the time, a fame greater than that enjoyed by the first of this small class of 5 locomotives. No. 903 was named *Cardean*, after the country estate of the Deputy Chairman of the Caledonian Board at that time, and in accordance with the practice of the day, so far as big engines on the Caledonian were concerned, it was allocated to one particular duty, and one only. *Cardean* had that veritable queen of Anglo-Scottish expresses, the 2 p.m. from Glasgow to Euston, which she took down to Carlisle. Then, after handing over to the L.&N.W.R., she brought the corresponding northbound express from Carlisle to Glasgow. And except for the very few occasions when she was under repair *Cardean* made that round trip every weekday for the best part of ten years! It was her unfailing reliability and excellent timekeeping that made the engine something of a legend – not only in Scotland but wherever there were railways. Technically *Cardean* and her four sister engines, none of which bore names, were a very large 4-6-0 development of the 'Dunalastairs', and their performance was enhanced in 1911–12 when they were fitted with superheaters. Simply and massively built, they were in every way an epitome of the neat, graceful British locomotives of the pre-1914 era.

104 Glasgow and South Western Railway; a Manson 4-6-0.

The Anglo-Scottish expresses following the Midland route from St Pancras to Carlisle were sharply timed, and greater engine power was needed than that afforded by the Manson 4-4-0s of 1892. The 4-6-0s built in 1903 were in every way a typical Manson design, in their neatness of outline and simplicity of detail. The drivers took to them at once, because they responded so readily to traditional methods of working between Glasgow and Carlisle. The new engines ran with the utmost freedom and steadiness downhill, and speeds of 85 m.p.h. and more were common. At the time these 4-6-0s were introduced there were no Pullman cars on the Anglo-Scottish trains; but since the inauguration of the through Midland service between St Pancras and Glasgow in 1876, the service to and from England was invariably referred to as the 'Pullmans'. The Manson 4-6-0s were economical engines on any count; but they were made even more so by the techniques of driving used by the men. At a later date two additional engines were built by Manson having superheaters, and these were probably the lightest engines on coal to be found anywhere in Great Britain at the time. All the Manson 4-6-0s passed into L.M.S.R. ownership; but by that time their day was practically over, and they were barely equal to the demands of the traffic.

105 The Highland 'Castle' Class.

David Jones, who had enjoyed so distinguished a career as Locomotive Superintendent of the Highland Railway since 1870, had the misfortune to sustain a serious injury on the footplate of one of his epoch-making 4-6-0 goods locomotives (see Plate 73). This so affected his health that he had to resign, many years before what would have been his normal retiring age. He had, however, prepared a design for an express passenger version of his famous goods 4-6-0, and it fell to his successor, Peter Drummond, to place this splendid engine in service. There was time for Drummond to include a number of the specialities for which he and his elder brother Dugald were well known, such as the steam reverser, compensated bogie, and the large double-bogie tender with inside frames. The boiler mountings and cab were those of the Drummonds. But in the fundamentals of the design the 'Castle' was a Jones product, and it was accorded the popularity common to every engine design Jones had produced while at Inverness. The 'Castle' class became the mainstay of the passenger service between Inverness and Perth, and remained so for nearly 20 years. A modified form of the class was introduced by F. G. Smith in 1913, and three more engines, with coupled wheels, 6 ft. diameter instead of 5 ft. 9 in. were built in 1917 to cope with the heavy wartime traffic on the Highland Railway. Our picture shows the original livery of 1900. In later years they were finished in plain green without any lining.

106 **A Reid 'Atlantic';** North British Railway.

In the early years of the twentieth century, as from its inception in 1876, the Midland and North British joint Anglo-Scottish service made heavy demands upon engine power between Edinburgh and Carlisle. In view of the gradients and the loads to be hauled a six-coupled engine would have seemed desirable; but because of the very bad curvature W. P. Reid decided upon an 'Atlantic', and he built the most powerful engine of the type ever to run in Great Britain. The first examples of the class were non-superheated, but after these had been modified their work became remarkable; both on the 'Waverley' route, and on the East Coast main line between Edinburgh and Aberdeen they took heavy loads, and climbed the

steep gradients with a sureness and efficiency that helped to make the North British one of the most punctual railways in Great Britain. These massive engines, which all had fine Scottish names, looked their best in the original North British brown livery; but in London and North Eastern days they remained among the selected few pre-grouping types to be painted in the new standard apple-green, when most others were relegated to 'black'. In all they put in thirty years' work on the Aberdeen route, though they were displaced from the Waverley route a little earlier.

107 **A Great Northern 'Atlantic'.**
Until the end of the Stirling régime Great Northern engines, despite the very fast and hard work they did on the line, were distinctly slender in appearance. Ivatt, in consequence, caused something of a surprise with his first 'Atlantic'; but that surprise was nothing compared with the veritable sensation that followed the building of his first 'large' Atlantic, No. 251, in 1902. The boiler and firebox were actually the only points of difference between No. 251 and the 'Klondykes' as the cylinders and all else remained the same. Although capable of very good work, the potentialities of these massive engines were not realized in their original state, and it was left to Ivatt's successor, the celebrated H. N. Gresley – later Sir Nigel Gresley – to make those modifications and additions that transformed them into truly wonderful engines. Gresley fitted them all with high-degree superheaters and some of them with slightly larger cylinders and piston valves. As such they could do extraordinary work. One of them ran the Queen of Scots Pullman from Leeds to Kings Cross in a net time of 176 min. for the run of 187 miles. while another of them, called upon to replace a disabled Pacific at Grantham at a moment's notice, ran the afternoon Scotsman over the 82¾ miles from

Grantham to York in 86½ min. with a very heavy train of *seventeen* bogie coaches, 585 tons. Our picture shows one of them in G.N.R. days. There was very little change externally, when they had been transformed by Sir Nigel Gresley.

108 **South Eastern and Chatham Railway;** Wainwright's 'E' class.

The working union of the South Eastern and the London Chatham and Dover Railways under a Managing Committee as from the year 1899 was accompanied by complete integration of the engineering and operating departments of the two former railways; and one outcome was the production of a range of very fine and exceedingly handsome locomotives, under the superintendence of H. S. Wainwright. The 4-4-0 of Class 'E' which is illustrated herewith was first introduced in 1905 and shared with the earlier engines of Class D all the heaviest work on both the former South Eastern and London Chatham and Dover routes until 1914. The Continental boat expresses, especially the mails, were heavy trains for that period, frequently loading up to 350 tons or more, and the 'E' class engines in particular did some excellent work with them. In a period when locomotives were still *objets d'art*, and cleaning was a ritual rather than a chore, the engines of the S.E.&C.R. were unusually ornate. One of the 'D' class has been preserved and is on show to the public in the Museum of Transport at Clapham. There one can study the beautiful painting and decorative work put into an ordinary workaday passenger locomotive of the early nineteen-hundreds.

109 **A Great Western 'Saint'.**

The standard G.W.R. express passenger two-cylinder 4-6-0 was the outcome of a classic locomotive development at Swindon. Churchward had set himself a performance target of a locomotive that would exert a drawbar pull of 2 tons at 70 m.p.h., and moreover a pull that could be sustained for an hour or more, if need be. The development took two definite lines: the designing of a boiler that would steam very freely, and would be trouble-free in service, albeit more expensive than a conventional one in first cost; a cylinder and valve gear that would use the steam to the best advantage. Most of the way towards these ideals had been attained when the second G.W.R. express 4-6-0 No. 98, was built at Swindon in 1903; but the final touch on a design-masterpiece was achieved with the third engine, No. 171, in which boiler pressure was increased to 225 lb. per sq. in. This engine gave a superior all-round performance to the French compound *La France*. The 'Saint' class came to include the original proto-type 4-6-0s; further engines of the same general type originally built as 'Atlantics'; the series named after 'Ladies', and the final 25 named after 'Courts'. The latter were built new with the Swindon super-heater, and all the earlier engines were similarly equipped in due course. Our picture shows engine No. 2914 *Saint Augustine*, as originally built, non-super-heated.

110 **A Midland Deeley Compound.**

The development and ultimate success of the 'Midland Compound' is one of the romances of British locomotive history. Leaving out of account its progenitor on the North Eastern Railway, W. M. Smith's patent locomotive of 1898, it went through four distinct phases: the original Smith-Johnson compound of 1902; the Deeley development of 1905; and the superheated rebuilds from 1913 onwards. These early varieties, which numbered 45 in all, had 7 ft. coupled wheels. Then, after grouping there came the L.M.S. development with 6 ft. 9 in. coupled wheels of which 195 were built. The variety chosen for illustration is the superheated compound, dating from 1913, when No. 1040, one of the original

Deeley engines was rebuilt by Sir Henry Fowler. The standard L.M.S. type will be noticed later on. The superheated compounds represent the highest development of express passenger locomotive practice on the Midland Railway. Between the time of the first rebuilding in 1913, and the summer of 1923 it was subject to various trials and modifications, but after the valve gear tests of March 1923 it was finalized as a magnificent motive power unit, particularly suitable to very hard work over the mountain gradients of the Derbyshire Peak District, and of the picturesque main line to Scotland between Settle and Carlisle.

111 A 'Jersey Lily' of the G.C.R.

In attempting to build up traffic on the London Extension line, in the face of severe competition from railways to east and to west, the Great Central used publicity in all its forms; one of these was to build 'prestige' locomotives. Certainly the actual demands of the traffic in the years 1903–4 did not demand anything so large or powerful as Robinson's beautiful 'Atlantics', though their excellent design and massive construction was to stand the L.N.E.R. in good stead 20 years later. The 'Atlantics' were nicknamed the 'Jersey Lilies'; but this allusion to the famous actress of the day, Lily Langtry, was not, as is sometimes thought, a tribute to the handsome appearance of the G.C.R. engines. The first of the class was a huge engine compared to everything that had gone before, and it so happened that at the time of its introduction one of the local public houses near Gorton Works included as one of its attractions an enormously fat woman, weighing, it is said, some 20 stones, and nicknamed, sarcastically, the 'Jersey Lily'. When the first Robinson 'Atlantic' took the road its vast size led to its being nicknamed immediately the 'Jersey Lily', and the engines were known thus throughout their existence. They were very fast and powerful engines, and ran the evening express from Marylebone to Bradford with great distinction until the year 1936.

112 The 'Great Bear'; Great Western Railway.

The great majority of the locomotives illustrated in this book have been representatives of large classes, or prototypes, the performance of which has had a marked influence on the future practice of the railway concerned. *The Great Bear*, designed by Churchward, and built at Swindon in 1908, was an outstanding case of a 'might-have-been'. It was built at a time when the G.W.R. was in the midst of a remarkable development programme in which great emphasis was laid on the production of large boilers that could be steamed efficiently, and which had low maintenance costs. *The Great Bear*, which remained the only British tender engine of the 'Pacific' type for a period of 14 years, had a steaming capacity far in advance of anything needed for the traffic of the day. It was more than a prestige symbol; it was a prototype built against the time when much larger locomotives might be required. That time never came during the period when Churchward was Chief Mechanical Engineer, and so 'The Bear', as it was affectionately known on the G.W.R., remained an isolated engine, and a difficult one to use to the best advantage. Because of its length and weight it was restricted to the main line between London and Bristol. In 1924 the boiler needed renewing; but because of the limited route availability of the engine it was decided to rebuild it as a 'Castle' class 4-6-0. The old number, 111, was retained, but it was renamed *Viscount Churchill* after the Chairman of the G.W.R.

113 A Brighton 'Atlantic'; L.B.& S.C.R.

Following the famous régime of William

Stroudley at Brighton the old traditions were carried on by his successor R. J. Billinton. But when the latter engineer was succeeded by D. Earle-Marsh, who had previously been on the Great Northern Railway, at Doncaster, there was a considerable change, and an early departure from previous practice was the introduction of some large Atlantic engines very similar in general appearance to H. A. Ivatt's large boilered Atlantics on the G.N.R. (reference 107). Five of these engines were put to work on the Brighton line at first, and did well in the haulage of seaside trains and residential expresses of ever increasing weight. They were followed by a superheated version of 1911. In the handsome dark brown livery they looked especially fine at the head of the 'Southern Belle', the all-Pullman 60-minute express between London and Brighton. After grouping of the railways in 1923 they were painted in the standard Southern livery of dark green, and at a later period they were all named, after headlands on the south coast of England. Some of these, such as *St Catherine's Point, The Needles, Hartland Point, Trevose Head* were excellent names; but on the other hand the name of engine No. 38, *Portland Bill*, had its unintentionally humorous side!

114 North Staffordshire Railway; John H. Adams's superheated tank engine.

The North Staffordshire Railway was primarily a local line serving the district indicated by its name. Much of its traffic originated in the Potteries, and the local services were excellently run. At the same time the Company had a very enterprising management, and a number of working arrangements with neighbouring companies led to extensive locomotive journeys well beyond the confines of the North Staffordshire. On holiday expresses N.S.R. locomotives worked as far afield as Llandudno. But one of the most interesting duties arose from the routing

of certain expresses between Manchester and London via the North Stafford line, so as to serve Macclesfield and Stoke-on-Trent, and on these important duties the North Staffordshire locomotives hauled the trains between Manchester and Stoke. These were heavy restaurant car expresses, and it was a point of honour with the N.S.R. drivers to hand the trains over to the London and North Western, at Stoke, on time. Adams designed the handsome 4-4-2 tank engines shown in our picture specially for these trains. The line is a hilly one, and in consequence the coupled wheels, were made rather smaller than usual for ordinary express working, namely 6 ft. instead of the more popular 6 ft. 6 in. to 6 ft. 9 in.

115 The 'Abergavenny'; Earle-Marsh's tank 4-6-2 engine.

A natural sequel to the success of the 'I3' class of 4-4-2 tank engine (reference 96), was the development of the design into something considerably larger to cope with the increasing loads of the fast trains between London and the South Coast towns. From the four-coupled 'I3' Marsh adopted the 4-6-2 wheel arrangement, in company with a much longer and larger boiler, and larger cylinders. The latter needed to be of a size such that they could not be accommodated within the frames, but in the tradition of that period the outside cylinders, crossheads and connecting rods were arranged very neatly, and a very handsome engine resulted. Only two of these engines were built, for trial purposes, one in 1910 and the other in 1912, and they differed from each other in respect of the valve gear. Engine No. 325 *Abergavenny*, as illustrated, had the Stephenson's link motion between the frames whereas No. 326 *Bessborough* had the Walschearts radial valve gear, outside. Both engines did excellent work, and but for Marsh's retirement they would probably have become the standard express locomotives for the line. But Marsh's successor, L. B. Billinton, introduced still larger tank engines in later years. Although *Abergavenny* and *Bessborough* remained thus an isolated pair of engines they had a long life and did much valuable work. They were still on the steam-hauled Tunbridge Wells trains in 1947–8, and were not scrapped until 1951.

116 The 'Immingham' Class 4-6-0; Great Central Railway.

J. G. Robinson, in the years between 1900 and 1912, provided the Great Central Railway with a series of locomotives for every kind of duty, and whether they were for the most spectacular main line express trains or for heavy mineral service, each was an artistic masterpiece, as well as a supremely good engineering job. In this period the Great Central Railway was developing trade with Scandinavia and with the Baltic, via Grimsby, and a great new port was under construction at Immingham Dock. In readiness for handling express goods traffic Robinson built a smaller wheeled variant of his 6 ft. 9 in. express passenger engines, some of which latter were of the 'Atlantic' type and some 4-6-0. The 'Immingham' class, as they were known, had 6 ft. 6 in. coupled wheels. Like Robinson's Atlantic (Jersey Lilies), these 4-6-0s were exceptionally strong and reliable engines. Their normal livery in Great Central days was black with a handsome amount of lining out in white and red, with the company's coat of arms on both engine and tender. In L.N.E.R. days the 'Imminghams' was painted apple green, and did much excellent work on the Kings Cross–Leeds expresses over the heavy gradients of the West Riding north of Doncaster, where the large Pacifics were not then allowed to run.

117 London Tilbury and Southern Railway; Thomas Whitelegg's express tank engine.

By the turn of the century residential traffic was rising to enormous proportions on the L.T.&S.R. line. The business trains were made up to the maximum length that could be accommodated in the platforms at Fenchurch Street station, and the most precise timekeeping prevailed. A late arrival of a Southend express had 'news value'. To keep abreast of traffic requirements Thomas Whitelegg reconstructed a batch of ten 4-4-2 tank engines originally put in service in 1897–8, giving them much larger boilers, new cylinders, and the very handsome appearance shown in our picture. These rebuilt engines did splendid work on the heavy business trains, and they were reinforced by four new engines to the same dimensions added to the stock in 1909. *Thundersley* was one of the 1909 batch, and was distinguished by having a polished casing to the safety valves. On all the other engines of the class this mounting was painted over green. The Midland Railway absorbed the Tilbury line in 1912, and after the former company had become part of the L.M.S. system in 1923 twenty-five more were built in 1923–7, and a final ten as comparatively recently as 1930. This in itself is a great tribute to the efficiency of Thomas Whitelegg's design of 1907.

118 The Class 'X' Hump shunters.

The North Eastern Railway was fortunate in having a very heavy coal traffic, and much of the output from the Durham and Northumberland coalfields was shipped from ports large and small along the North-east coast. At the points of heaviest concentration hump marshalling yards were laid in, and there shunting engines of exceptional power were needed. Wilson Worsdell, in his handsome Class 'X' shunters, followed the precedent set two years earlier on the Great Central Railway by using three-cylinder propulsion. This provided a very even starting effort, and enabled the locomotive to propel a heavy train from rest without slipping, and jerking. Ten of these engines were built in 1909–10, and a further five were built by the L.N.E.R. in 1925 – a sure proof of their great success. The earlier ones put in more than 45 years' work. Each engine used to be in continuous service for 24 hours at a stretch, and their bunker capacity of 3 tons was enough to provide all the fuel for this long term of duty. They had one very interesting constructional feature that was later adopted by Sir Nigel Gresley in some of his modern L.N.E.R. three-cylinder locomotives, in that the three cylinders and their associated valve chests were made in a single casting. This in itself was a fine tribute to the foundry techniques in use at Gateshead works.

119 The 'Coronation' Engine of 1911; London and North Western Railway.

These engines, designed and built at Crewe under the direction of C. J. Bowen-Cooke, are sometimes dismissed as nothing more than a superheated version of the Whale 'Precursor'. It is true that the chassis, wheels, boiler barrel, and firebox were the same; but the application of the Schmidt superheater was accompanied by a re-design of the cylinders, and by the use of piston valves instead of slide valves, and the improvement in haulage capacity and thermal efficiency was very striking. In relation to their size and weight the 90 engines of this class did some phenomenal work. It was nothing unusual for them to take trains of 390 tons behind the tender up the 1 in 75 of Shap Incline without assistance, and at the southern end of the line they would make start-to-stop average speeds of 55 to 58 m.p.h. between Euston and Crewe with loads up to 450 tons. By the standards of 1910–1916 – their hey-day – they were economical in fuel and repairs, though in recognition of the very hard work they were called upon

to do the day-to-day maintenance was very good. Because of the success of the 'George the Fifth' class many of the non-superheated 'Precursors' were rebuilt, with piston valves, superheaters and extended smokeboxes, making them identical to the 'George the Fifths' in everything except the quite superficial difference of the separate splasher for the leading pair of coupled wheels, instead of the continuous splasher.

120 A Great Central 'Director'.

The introduction of superheating led many locomotive engineers towards consideration of smaller engines to do the work previously entrusted to 'Atlantics' and 4-6-0s, and the Great Central 'Director' class, of 1913, was an expression of this trend. These engines were designed to work through between London and Manchester, whereas the 'Atlantics' had usually to be changed at intermediate points. The first ten, built in 1913, were all named after directors of the company, though in the course of their long life two were re-named. Another 11 of a slightly enlarged design were built by the Great Central Railway in 1920, and it is one of these, No. 506 *Butler-Henderson* that has been preserved, and is housed in the Museum of Transport at Clapham. After grouping, another 24 of these fine engines were built specially for service in Scotland. Because of the reduced height of the loading gauge on the former North British Railway the Scottish engines had very much reduced chimneys and boiler mountings, and did not look so handsome in consequence. They all had names taken from characters in the Waverley novels, such as *Flora MacIvor*, *Haystoun of Bucklaw*, *Wizard of the Moor*, and *The Fiery Cross*. The original 'Directors' continued to do excellent work on the old Great Central line down to the year 1936, while the Scottish variants worked between Edinburgh, Dundee, Perth and Glasgow.

121 **Midland Railway;** Fowler's Class 2 superheated 4-4-0.

The traffic policy of the Midland Railway from the year 1907 onwards was to run a frequent service of fast, lightly loaded trains on all main routes, and because this did not demand the building of large new locomotives a programme was initiated for modernizing many of the older 4-4-0s of Johnson's of the type illustrated on Plate 60. In Deeley's time a number of these engines were rebuilt with larger boilers of similar design to those provided for the Somerset and Dorset 4-4-0s built at Derby in 1903, and illustrated on Plate 85. But from 1913 onwards a further stage in modernization was commenced, with the production, on the old chassis, and using the same wheels and motion, of a superheated rebuild, with a still larger boiler. Within their power class these proved excellent engines. Naturally they were limited in the loads they could take, but with this reservation they were fast, efficient, and very light on repairs. They worked all over the Midland system, including the heavy road from Leeds to Carlisle, and after the grouping of the railways the design formed the basis of a new L.M.S.R. standard, for light passenger working, having 6 ft. 9 in. coupled wheels against the 7 ft. of the Midland No. 2 Class engines. The Midland 7 ft. design was adopted for express passenger working on the Somerset and Dorset Joint Railway, and some engines of the design were painted in the handsome blue livery of that railway, and bore the initials S.D.J.R. on their tenders.

122 **Dugald Drummond's 'D15';** L.&S.W.R.

Following the conspicuous success of his 'T9' 'small' 4-4-0s Dugald Drummond built several classes of 4-4-0 for the L.&S.W.R. with larger boilers, and the class chosen for illustration is the 'D15', of which 10 were built in 1912. These very handsome engines included all the features of the 'T9' class, and as originally built they had the firebox water tubes. Like the 'T9s' they were very fast runners, but the enlarged boiler and proportions did not seem to give them as much extra capacity as was expected, and they did not really come into their own until Drummond's successor, R. W. Urie, fitted them with Eastleigh superheaters, accompanied by an extended smokebox. Their very graceful appearance at the front end was somewhat impaired, but their performance was vastly improved. The 'D15' class was the last of a group of three large-boilered 4-4-0s of Drummond design, of which the others were the smaller-wheeled 'S11' class, designed for working on the hilly routes west of Exeter, and the 'L12', built in 1904-5. These latter were really a modified version of the 'T9', having the same chassis and machinery but with a larger boiler. In appearance they were very similar to the 'D15' class. Both the 'L12' and the 'D15' classes were long-lived; all the engines of both classes worked throughout the second World War, and passed into the ownership of the nationalized British Railways in 1948.

123 **Great Eastern Railway;** The '1500' class 4-6-0.

For twelve strenuous years the 'Claud Hamilton' class 4-4-0s did excellent and most reliable work on the heaviest Great Eastern passenger services. So far as they were concerned the adjective 'heavy' was no mere comparative term. In the summer holiday season the express trains from London to Yarmouth and Cromer were among the heaviest in Great Britain. Then, in 1912, Stratford Works brought out the splendid superheater 4-6-0. This could be described as an enlarged 'Claud Hamilton', and the new engines very quickly proved themselves very strong and free-running. They were put on to the Norfolk Coast Express, and the

Continentals, and did very fine work from the outset. But some of their finest performance took place after the end of World War I when pre-war speed was restored, with still heavier loads. The work of the link of drivers at Parkeston Quay on the Hook of Holland boat express will live in locomotive history. In later years many of them were transferred to the former Great North of Scotland line, for service between Aberdeen and Elgin, and on the fish trains from the Buchan ports. Although the earliest engines of the class carried the beautiful G.E.R. blue livery shown in our picture, this was not restored after the war. Instead they ran in a plain unlined slate grey, until the grouping, after which they looked bright and cheerful again in the L.N.E.R. apple green.

124 A North Eastern 'Z'.

From the beginning of the twentieth century a variety of large ten-wheeled engines for express passenger traffic were built by the North Eastern Railway. There were 4-6-os, two-cylinder 'Atlantics', and two experimental four-cylinder compound 'Atlantics'; and in 1908 there was even a reversion to the 4-4-0 type, in the very large and powerful 'R1' class. What proved, however, to be the company's standard large express passenger engine appeared in 1911, in the form of the handsome three-cylinder simple 4-4-2 of the 'Z' class. These engines combined the high steaming capacity of a boiler with an outside diameter of 5 ft. 6 in., with the smoothness of action of a multi-cylindered layout. The result was that they ran well, pulled very heavy loads, and were much appreciated by the men for their comfort and smoothness in travelling. On the fine racing stretch of the East Coast main line between Darlington and York they took the Anglo-Scottish expresses of 350 to 400 tons at sustained speeds of well over 70 m.p.h., and there are recorded instances of loads,

taken punctually and without assistance, of up to 550 tons on the standard schedules of the day. They were still engaged on first-class express work up to the summer of 1934. A total of fifty was built, and historically they rank as one of the finest sets of engines designed and built for service in the North-East of England.

125 A 'Prince of Wales' 4-6-0; London and North Western.

These engines, like the 4-4-0 'George the Fifth' class, were a superheated development of a Whale design, and they proved the most generally useful passenger class the L.&N.W.R. ever possessed. At the time of grouping of the railways at the end of 1922 the company had no fewer than 245 of them in service. In their early days they were classified for traffic purposes as the same as the 'George the Fifths', and indeed there was little to choose between the maximum efforts of the two classes. The 'Prince of Wales' was quite a small 4-6-0, though it was potentially the more powerful of the two classes in having a somewhat larger boiler and firebox. The 'Prince of Wales' became generally favoured on the heavy gradients of the line between Lancaster and Carlisle, and by the time of grouping it was rare to see a 'George the Fifth' north of Preston. Engines of the 'Prince of Wales' class were engaged in competitive trials against Midland, Caledonian, and Lancashire and Yorkshire engines after the grouping. Although they did well so far as weight haulage was concerned the coal consumption was greater than that of the Midland compounds. The first 90 of the engines were named, in the old tradition of the L.& N.W.R. But in the difficult days after the end of World War I, when brass was in short supply, naming was discontinued in the 155 engines built after the war. These engines were turned out in plain black, without any lining, and the only adornment was the company's crest on the splashers.

126 A Drummond 4-Cylinder 4-6-0; L.&S.W.R.

As a locomotive designer Dugald Drummond was outstandingly successful with his smaller engines, but his essays into machines of greater power were beset by difficulties. The engine illustrated, however, was one of a class that did some good and very fast running on the West of England and Bournemouth routes. By reason of their very large splashers with the circular inspection cover they were nicknamed the 'Paddleboats' – the splashers being referred to as the 'paddleboxes'. Their performance on the crack trains were variable, but this was in some measure due to the rather awkward technique required in firing, rather than to any inherent fault in the basic design. The firebox was large, and very shallow, and great care was needed in spreading the coal evenly beneath the brick arch. Like all Drummond engines they were handsomely proportioned, though at a time when the majority of engineers were adopting superheaters Drummond was content with his own 'steam dryer', which raised the temperature of the steam to no more than 400 deg. Fah., where other engineers were using temperatures of 550 to 600 deg. Fah. The 'Paddleboats' were twice modernized: first by Urie, who fitted them with Eastleigh superheaters, and secondly in Southern Railway days by R. E. L. Maunsell, who followed his own dictum of making everything get-at-able by removing the 'paddlebox' splashers, and fitting forced lubrication for the coupled wheel axleboxes.

127 A North Western 'Claughton'.

Herculean though the work of the superheated express locomotives of the 'George the Fifth' and 'Prince of Wales' classes was in the years 1910–13, C. J. Bowen-Cooke had no sooner succeeded George Whale as Chief Mechanical Engineer than he was planning a far larger express locomotive than either of the two previously mentioned classes. It was a time when most locomotive engineers were restricted by the dead weight they could carry on any one axle, but Bowen-Cooke hoped to secure some relaxation in this respect by designing an engine in which the reciprocating parts were perfectly balanced. Following the practice that had developed in South Germany, where he had been very impressed by some 4-cylinder compound 4-6-0s on the Bavarian Railways, Bowen-Cooke arranged for all four cylinders in his new design to drive on to the leading axle. He secured a very smooth and fast running engine; but relaxation of weight restrictions was not forthcoming, and the 'Sir Gilbert Claughton' class had smaller boilers than was originally intended. Nevertheless they did some fine work, and it is a tribute to their success that no fewer than 130 were built. They needed a careful technique in firing, and with inexpert treatment in this respect they steamed poorly. But with proper handling their feats of weight haulage at high speed were unsurpassed in Great Britain up to the end of World War I, and they took loads up to 440 tons unassisted on the Shap incline.

128 L. Billinton's Giant 4-6-4.

The ultimate development of express passenger locomotive power on the Brighton railway is represented by L. Billinton's 4-6-4 tank design, of which the first examples were built in 1914. These engines were intended to provide an ample, almost overwhelming amount of power for the South Coast trains, so that a high average speed could be maintained without excessive maximum speed downhill. Only two of these huge engines were built at first. The incidence of war, in 1914, halted the traffic developments that made them desirable. Of the original engines No. 327 was named *Charles C. Macrae*, but the second remained nameless. After the war further engines of the class were built and the last of the series, No. 333, was notable in being finished specially in grey, and given the name *Remembrance*, in honour of the men of the L.B.&S.C.R. who fell in World War I. After grouping the remaining engines of the class, Nos. 327 to 332 were renamed after locomotive engineers famous in the early history of the constituent companies of the Southern Railway. At a still later period, when all the main lines of the former Brighton railway had been electrified, these one-time 4-6-4 tanks were converted to 4-6-0 tender engines, and continued to do good work on the former London and South Western section of the Southern Railway.

129 A Great Northern 'Mogul'.

The first Great Northern 'Mogul' engines, of 1912, caused a considerable stir in the locomotive world, but while they did good work on fast goods trains Gresley found they had insufficient boiler capacity for the heavy mixed traffic duties envisaged, and in 1914 he built a new series, similar so far as the cylinders and machinery were concerned, but with a much larger boiler. These proved to be splendid engines, and no fewer than 65 were built. In addition to fast goods services they also worked on passenger trains. Though having driving wheels no larger than 5 ft. 8 in. diameter they were fast runners, and frequently exceeded 70 m.p.h. Our picture shows one of them in the G.N.R. passenger livery, in which they originally appeared. They were painted in the goods grey after World War I and still later in L.N.E.R. black. In the nineteen-thirties a number of them were transferred to Scotland. These were fitted with enlarged cabs, giving a better protection against the

weather, and thirteen of them working on the magnificently-scenic West Highland line were named after lochs lying within sight, or relatively near to the railway. These Scottish 2-6-0s put in many years of very hard work on this steeply graded and sharply curved route. Although in many ways so different from the indigenous Scottish locomotives they became great favourites with the enginemen from their solid reliability.

130 A 'River' Class 4-6-0.

When Peter Drummond secured the post of Locomotive Superintendent of the Glasgow and South Western Railway in 1913, he was succeeded by F. G. Smith, who had been Works Manager at Inverness since 1905. Smith was a first-rate locomotive engineer, and immediately began to make plans for a new passenger engine design that would once more put the Highland Railway ahead of all the other Scottish companies for both power and efficiency. But by some extraordinary mischance certain civil engineering restrictions had been overlooked; they were, in fact, not fully appreciated until the first of the engines had actually arrived at Perth, from the builders' works in Newcastle. It was only then found inadvisable to run the engines on the Highland Railway, and they were sold to the Caledonian. Our picture shows one of these engines in the livery of the latter company, for which they did good work for 12 years. After grouping, when the civil engineering restrictions had been removed, the six engines were put on to the Highland section, and they took up the work they were originally intended to do. It is a sad story, because in 1928 the locomotives that would have been a tremendous asset to the Highland Railway in 1915 were becoming obsolescent. Nevertheless they were able to show their mettle, albeit belatedly, and were at once accorded their original class name, the 'Rivers', by the men. On the Caledonian they were always known as the 'Highlandmen'.

131 Churchward's Masterpiece; the Great Western 4-cylinder 'Star' class.

The 'Star' class was the outcome of a most important series of experiments and researches at Swindon Works, during which the latest features of American and French locomotive practice were studied. (See also the *La France* reference 97.) The 'Star' embodied the divided drive, as in the French compound, but with all four cylinders taking high pressure steam. It had the same outstanding boiler as the 'Saint', using 225 lb. per sq. in. in pressure, and an interesting detail of French practice in the de Glehn big-end for the inside cylinder connecting rods. The 'Stars', of which 72 were built between 1907 and 1922, did magnificent work in traffic. One of their finest feats was that of the *King Richard*, No. 4026, in 1925, hauling an up West of England express weighing no less than 550 tons from Taunton to Paddington, 143 miles in 152 min. Successive batches of the 'Stars' were named after 'Knights', 'Kings', 'Queens', 'Princes', 'Princesses' and 'Abbeys'. No. 4003 *Lode Star* is preserved in the Great Western Railway Museum at Swindon. The 'Star' formed the basis of design of the still larger 'Castles' and 'Kings' of the G.W.R.

132 A Pickersgill 4-4-0; Caledonian Railway.

These handsome engines, of which 48 were built between the years 1916 and 1922, were a development of the famous 'Dunalastair' family of engine classes introduced by J. F. McIntosh. In the new engines, although the likenesses to their predecessors was strong, there were numerous relatively small evidences that a different personality was in charge at St Rollox Works. Moreover, Pickersgill was not a Caledonian man, but one who had previously held the post of Locomo-

tive Superintendent on the Great North of Scotland Railway. There he had been responsible for some excellent, though small 4-4-0s. Nevertheless the 'Pickersgill bogies' on the Caledonian included much detail design that had been traditional at St Rollox from the days of Dugald Drummond, and some items could be traced back to Drummond's association with Stroudley at Brighton, more than forty years before the appearance of the Pickersgill 4-4-0s. They did some hard work on all parts of the Caledonian main line, and with the stud eventually numbering 48 locomotives they were the largest passenger class numerically on the line. Many of them were still hard at work in Scotland forty years after their first introduction, and some of them were still on the active list as recently as the autumn of 1961.

133 Glasgow and South Western Railway; Peter Drummond's express goods.

The Drummond brothers between them made a very notable contribution to British locomotive practice, serving four Scottish and one English railway. On the Highland Railway the younger brother, Peter, followed closely along the lines of Dugald Drummond's work; but his transfer to the Glasgow and South Western Railway came almost at the same time as Dugald's death, and the period from 1912 to 1918 at Kilmarnock thus represents the final phase of the Drummond school of design. Many details were at once changed from the practice of James Manson, including that always-controversial point, the position of the driver on the footplate. The G.&S.W.R. had always driven from the right-hand side; the Drummonds insisted on left-hand drive. But details apart, Peter Drummond provided the Glasgow and South Western Railway with some excellent main line engines: 0-6-0 goods, 4-4-0 passenger, and then a superheated development of the 0-6-0. Because of the increased weight at the front end a pony-truck was inserted, thus making the superheated goods a 2-6-0. These engines had all the traditional neatness of a Drummond design, but with the massiveness of a machine suited to twentieth-century needs, and moreover that of a heavy wartime traffic. These 2-6-0s did excellent and economical work and many of them were still in service in the early nineteen-thirties.

134 A North British 'Glen'; West Highland line.

The locomotive department of the North British Railway, like that of the rival Caledonian had been given a tremendous fillip by the fine 4-4-0s designed for them by Dugald Drummond, and at Cowlairs, as at St Rollox, the Drummond design formed a basis for the developments of many years thereafter. W. P. Reid built some powerful express passenger 4-4-0s with names taken from characters in the 'Waverley' novels, and he followed those with a so-called 'intermediate' class, unnamed, with 6 ft. diameter coupled wheels. It was when these were followed by a superheated version of the same series that Reid produced one of the most outstandingly successful 4-4-0s ever to run in Scotland. They were intended particularly for the West Highland line, with its incessant curvature and 1 in 60 gradients extending from Helensburgh on the Firth of Clyde, to Fort William and Mallaig, and the engines were all named after glens, lying on or near the route. They proved ideal engines for this strenuous duty. They could be pounded up the long gradients without the slightest ill-effects; they steamed freely, and suffered no trouble from the heating of bearings that might have been expected on so severe a route. To travel in a long train of 11 or 12 coaches hauled by a pair of them was an experience never to be forgotten.

135 Somerset and Dorset Joint Railway; one of the special freight engines.

In meeting the responsibility for providing and maintaining locomotive power for this very difficult route the Midland Railway had to cope with grading conditions far worse than anything on their own line. Under reference 85, mention was made of a new type of 4-4-0 which with suitable adaptation subsequently became a Midland Railway standard; and again, in 1914, the Derby drawing office designed, for the S.D.J.R., a freight engine larger and more powerful than anything used on the Midland Railway proper. These very successful 2-8-0s, which came to put in nearly 50 years' service on the Somerset and Dorset line, were to some extent a synthesis of standard parts. They used the boiler of the standard superheated compound 4-4-0, though of course the use of outside cylinders and Walschaerts valve gear was new to Midland practice. To provide tractive power for hauling the freight trains on the 1 in 50 banks the cylinders were very large, 21 in. diameter by 28 in. stroke. and these could not easily have been accommodated inside. In their last years these engines, surprisingly enough, have done a considerable amount of passenger working, on summer Saturdays. Their high tractive power has enabled them to take heavier trains without assistance than the modern 4-6-0s, and this was invaluable at a time when there was a serious shortage of locomotives.

136 Caledonian Railway; a Pickersgill 4-6-0 of 1916.

From the time of Dugald Drummond, who came to St Rollox in 1882, the Caledonian had been a line of inside-cylinder locomotives. Considerable interest was aroused in 1916 when the new locomotive engineer, W. Pickersgill, from the Great North of Scotland Railway, put on the road a series of six new 4-6-0s with outside cylinders. Dimensionally they could be regarded as a half-way house between two varieties of large-boilered McIntosh 4-6-0: the 5 ft. 9 in. express goods class and the famous express passenger 'Cardeans' (reference 103). But Pickersgill introduced many changes in detail, as well as the change to outside cylinders, and these handsome and powerful engines never established any particular reputation for *speed*. They steamed well, and climbed the banks in excellent style. Furthermore they were so strongly and soundly constructed that they were very light on repair costs. This feature attracted the attention of the L.M.S.R. management, and a further batch of these Caledonian engines was built in 1925 after the grouping of the railways. One of these latter was put through a series of tests between Carlisle and Preston in 1926, and gave quite satisfactory results. The post-grouping engines of this class were painted Midland red when new; but at a later date, as mixed traffic engines they were painted plain black.

137 A 'Super D' 0-8-0 Goods; London and North Western Railway.

Whatever success may have attended the running of the Webb compound 0-8-0 coal engines, when new locomotives were required, after Webb's retirement, his successors turned to a simple two-cylinder 0-8-0 with a large boiler, and a very straightforward cylinder and valve layout. There came to be many varieties of this excellent and long-lived class, all having their own distinguishing class letters; but the general term by which the engines were known among the men was derived from Whale's first rebuild, with large boiler, of the Webb three-cylinder compound coal engines. These were non-super-heated, and were known as Class 'D'. When the superheater version of this class appeared in 1912 it was no more

than natural to call it a 'Super D', though the actual class name was 'G1'. At the time the L.&N.W.R. was merged into the L.M.S.R. system there were 295 of these engines, including some with higher boiler pressure classed officially as 'G2'. As a willing, reliable work-horse of a locomotive the 'Super Ds' have scarcely been surpassed. They were in their element hauling trains of 800 to 900 tons on the main line between Preston – Crewe and London; but in emergency they were sometimes put on to passenger trains and a record exists of one of them running up to 58 m.p.h. with a fast express between Watford and Euston.

138 North Staffordshire Railway; Hookham's passenger tank engine.

The increasing weight of the Manchester–London expresses running via Stoke constituted something of a problem for the North Staffordshire locomotive department. Notwithstanding the fine work done by the Adams 4-4-2 tanks, a four-coupled engine was not ideal for such a steeply graded route, and in consequence J. A. Hookham designed a six-coupled engine with ample boiler capacity. It is interesting that he should have chosen the 0-6-4 type, because on some other railways engines of this wheel-arrangement had not been notably successful, or smooth in riding at express speed. The North Staffordshire engines on the Manchester–London expresses had not only to climb well, particularly on the heavy ascent that comes immediately after the restart at Macclesfield, but they had to run freely at speeds of over 60 m.p.h. The allowance for the 19.9 miles from Macclesfield to Stoke was only 27 min. The big 0-6-4 tanks did their work well, and amply upheld the reputation of the North Staffordshire Railway. It is notable that the locomotive department at Stoke produced two engineers that came to render most distinguished service to the L.M.S.R. First there was T. Coleman, who became Chief Draughtsman to Sir William Stanier, and who worked out the design of the 'Coronation' Pacific of 1937, and then there was H. G. Ivatt, the last Chief Mechanical Engineer of the L.M.S.R. Both were at one time North Staffordshire men.

139   A North Eastern 'T2'.

As a line with so heavy a coal traffic the North Eastern had an excellent record of heavy mineral engine performance. From Fletcher's 0-6-0s, and the Worsdell von Borries compounds of Class 'C', the younger Worsdell introduced eight-coupled coal engines in 1901. It is remarkable to recall that when first built these splendid, hard-slogging 'colliers' were decked in the full passenger engine livery of pale green, smartly lined out, and with polished brass safety valve casings. They did a great deal of tremendously hard work, and in due course they were followed, in 1913, by a superheated version, with still larger boilers. By that time the finish of freight engines was much plainer, and the 'T2' class, as they were designated, was in plain black, without any lining. They were considerably less handsome in outline. But if ever a locomotive class has earned its keep, in hard, unobtrusive, continuous duty, it is the North Eastern 'T2'. Altogether 120 of them were put into service between 1913 and 1921. There was no finesse about the working of these engines; they were down-to-earth freighters, that clanged and banged their way along. But they were utterly reliable, and after doing yeoman service in the 1939–45 emergency they were often referred to as 'the engines that won the war'.

140   A Highland Railway 'Clan'.

The Highland Railway should have added to its stock six exceptionally large and well-designed 4-6-0 locomotives in 1915. The mischance that led to their not being put into service has been told

(reference 130) and as a wartime expediency recourse was had to more 'Castles'. But the new locomotive superintendent, Christopher Cumming, designed some excellent new 4-6-0s, the first four of which were put into service in 1919. While including modern features new to the Highland Railway, such as Walschearts valve gear, superheaters, and Belpaire fireboxes they were nevertheless built in the well-established traditions of Inverness, which required an engine that would steam constantly while being pounded, for half an hour or more, up the heavy gradients of the Perth-Inverness line. The new engines, named after some of the greatest of the Highland clans, fulfilled this need admirably, and put in many years of hard work. After grouping when larger engines of English design were put on to the Highland section of the L.M.S.R. the eight engines of the 'Clan' class were transferred to the former Caledonian line to Oban. This was a route in many ways more severe than the Highland itself, and one which was in need of powerful and reliable engines. The 'Clans', still carrying their honoured names, became great favourites with the Oban men, and proved so useful that the last of them, the *Clan Mackinnon*, not was withdrawn from service till 1949.

141   The Gresley 'K3' 2-6-0.

This was originally a Great Northern design, introduced by Gresley in 1920. It was the first class on which the standard form of the Gresley conjugated valve gear was used, in which only two sets of the gear are required to actuate the valves of all three cylinders. The original batch, G.N.R. Nos. 1000–1009, were painted in the standard 'passenger green' livery, with the handsome lining out, and light red underframes. They also had the old style of G.N.R. cab, as on the 'K2' Moguls. But when the design was adopted as an L.N.E.R. standard, and many more locomotives were built, up to a total for the class of nearly 200, they were finished in the black lined livery. The tenders varied in detail. The one illustrated is that fitted to the original G.N.R. engines. They were general utility machines in every way, hauling heavy goods, express passenger of a class below that of the top link Pacifics, and proving very speedy and economical. Although the coupled wheels were no more than 5 ft. 8 in. diameter they frequently attained speeds of 75 m.p.h. Perhaps their finest work was done on the through fully-fitted express goods train services of the L.N.E.R. The afternoon 'Scotch Goods' from Kings Cross was booked to average 45 m.p.h. non-stop over the 112 miles from Peterborough to York, and on this duty the 'K3s' were scheduled to take a load of 55 wagons.

142 **South Eastern and Chatham Railway;** Maunsell's 'N' class.
The retirement of Wainwright in 1913 led to a complete reorganization of the locomotive department of the S.E.&C.R. and although war conditions imposed serious restrictions upon all development work Maunsell and his staff did manage to produce, during the war, two new locomotives that proved the prototypes of much new construction afterwards. One of these was the 'N' class 2-6-0, a powerful general-utility design, which showed the influence of Great Western practice in the tapered boiler barrel, and the use of a long-lap, long-travel layout in the valve gear. In exterior design the pioneer 'N' class engine No. 810, had the plain, essentially functional look that characterized Maunsell's work in S.E.& C.R. days. Engine No. 810 was a great success in fast goods and intermediate passenger working, and multiplication of the design began soon after the end of the war. The 'N' class became a Southern Railway standard, and formed the basis of a development of a family of similar engines, some with larger wheels, designed for light express traffic on heavily graded

routes. The 'N' class had been used all over the Southern Railway system, and until 1945 it was responsible for the heaviest passenger workings west of Exeter. Although steam is being replaced so rapidly many of these engines are still in service today.

143 **A Maunsell 'E1'** 4-4-0; S.E.& C.R.
Immediately after the end of the First World War the management of the S.E.&C.R. took a decision to concentrate in future all boat train traffic upon Victoria Station. This at once created a serious problem for the locomotive department, because civil engineering restrictions on the Chatham line precluded use of the powerful superheated 4-4-0s of 'L' class which had been introduced in 1914. Nothing larger than the non-superheated 'D' and 'E' class were permitted, and these would not have been able to handle the 300-ton trains required by the traffic department. R. E. L. Maunsell, who had succeeded Wainwright in 1913, thereupon carried out a very clever rebuilding of one of the 'E' class engines, No. 179: fitting a superheater, modernizing the design of the valve gear, and cutting down weight wherever possible. The result was an engine of considerably enhanced capacity that was no heavier than the original engine. The secret of success lay in the valve gear, but at the same time the engine was given an entirely 'new look'. In the austere livery of wartime there could not be greater contrast between these rebuilt engines and the originals, decked in all their finery (reference 108). Looks apart, the rebuilds were, for their size, some of the finest working engines ever to run in Great Britain.

144 **Furness Railway;** E. Sharples's 4-6-4 tank engine.
Apart from the mail trains, and the connections to London and North Western

long-distance expresses at Carnforth, most of the passenger working on the Furness Railway consisted of smartly-timed stopping trains. Before the large-scale introduction of private motoring there was a surprising amount of station-to-station passenger business. Various types of locomotives were used ranging from Pettigrew's latest 4-4-0s, to 0-6-2 tank engines, and after World War I the need was felt for larger engines. On short runs a tank engine has a considerable advantage, and E. Sharples prepared designs for the neat and powerful 4-6-4 that is illustrated. Much larger than anything that had preceded them on the Furness Railway these engines made short work of all kinds of traffic. They accelerated from rest with great rapidity, and ran freely at speeds of 50 to 55 m.p.h. They were well liked for their smooth riding and easy action, but their life in the Furness Railway livery was short. After grouping they were painted in Midland red, and as such looked very handsome; but after a short time 'red' was reserved only for the top-link express locomotives, and all other classes were painted in black. But whether in 'iron-ore' red, 'Midland red', or black, the 'Big Jumbos', as they were known, filled a very useful niche in Furness Railway operating.

145 The Lickey Bank Engine; Midland Railway.

The Lickey Incline has always formed a very formidable obstacle in the path of northbound trains on the West of England main line of the Midland Railway. The gradient is 1 in 37½ for 2 miles between Bromsgrove and Blackwell, and while 4-4-0 engines of the No. 2 Class would bring loads of 250 tons or even more up from Bristol, substantial assistance in rear was always needed up the Lickey Incline. A number of 0-6-0 tank engines were kept in steam at Bromsgrove to assist every north-bound train, pas-

senger and goods alike, and with the heavier trains two and sometimes even three bank engines were necessary. The 10-coupled tender engine, nicknamed 'Big Bertha', was designed as an experiment: as a machine that would do the work of two 0-6-0 engines. She was by far the largest and heaviest locomotive ever built by the Midland Railway, and fully justified the claims made for her. It certainly needed careful management of the fire before an ascent to keep those four large cylinders adequately supplied with steam during the 7 or 8 minutes of heavy pounding up the incline. But from her construction in 1919, she did the job for 30 years. She must have been unique among main line engines in having so limited a sphere of activity. All her work throughout those 30 years was done between Bromsgrove South and Blackwell – a distance of less than 3 miles. The only times when she went further afield were her periodic visits to Derby Works for overhaul.

146 The 'N2' Suburban Tank of 1921; Great Northern Railway.

The London suburban lines of the Great Northern Railway are uniformly difficult for the operation of heavy and fast passenger traffic. The immediate start out of Kings Cross is severely graded, and while the main line continues to Potters Bar on a long steady incline of 1 in 200 the branches, and particularly that to High Barnet, are very much more severe. Again, the City Widened Lines, of the Metropolitan Railway, over which Great Northern trains work between Kings Cross and Moorgate, required locomotives to condense their exhausts in the tunnels, and the climb between Kings Cross (underground) and the main line, in tunnel throughout and round the severe 'Hotel Curve', is a very awkward piece of railway. In H. A. Ivatt's time, 8-coupled tank engines were tried for a time, but ultimately the 0-6-2 type prevailed, and it was in producing a powerful superheated development of the Ivatt 0-6-2 that Gresley secured such marked success, in 1921. Sixty of them were put into service in that year, all fitted with the prominent condensing pipes on the side of the boiler. To such an extent were these engines on top of their job that they outlasted steam in the London area of the L.N.E.R. and all put in some forty years of hard work. After grouping of the railways, a further batch, without condensing apparatus, were built for service on the L.N.E.R. suburban lines around Edinburgh and Glasgow.

147 Great Northern Railway; Gresley's 3-cylinder 2-8-0.

The Great Northern, from its very inception, was a line of long-haul heavy goods and mineral traffic. Archibald Sturrock first tackled the problem with his famous but unsuccessful steam tenders (reference 24). H. A. Ivatt very quickly adopted eight coupled engines, which Gresley developed, with much larger boilers, into a 2-8-0. The first batch of these had two cylinders, outside; but having regard to the very heavy trains regularly worked, and the need frequently for starting on a heavy gradient, Gresley felt that a 3-cylinder layout would give smoother and easier starting, and in conjunction with these he developed his well-known conjugated valve gear, in which only two sets of motion are needed to actuate the valves of all three cylinders. A first and rather complicated version of this arrangement was fitted to one 2-8-0 engine, No. 461, in 1918, but the finalized gear was incorporated in the '02' class of 1921 beginning with engine No. 477. These locomotives proved ideal for the heavy coal traffic from South Yorkshire and Nottingham to London, and eventually more than fifty were built. The earliest examples were painted in the standard Great Northern 'freight-grey', as shown in our picture. The later ones, built after the grouping, had modified cabs, giving a much better protection from the weather.

148 R. Whitelegg's Baltic Tank; Glasgow and South Western Clyde coast services.

Robert Whitelegg was the son of the Locomotive Superintendent of the London Tilbury and Southend Railway, and was brought up in the tradition of the handsome engines and impeccable service referred to in connection with plate 117. He duly succeeded his father in office on the L.T.S.R., and built some remarkable tank engines of the 'Baltic' (4-6-4) type. But after the L.T.S.R. was taken over by the Midland he resigned, and went to the Glasgow and South Western after the death of Peter Drummond, in 1918. There he repeated his earlier essay in 'Baltic' tank engine design, though on a still more powerful scale. Once again, however, he had no sooner produced his great engines than the railway concerned was absorbed in a far larger combination – this time whe the G.&S.W.R. passed into the L.M.S.R. group. Rather than remain as a mere divisional chief Whitelegg resigned to become General Manager of the famous locomotive building firm of Beyer, Peacock and Co. The Glasgow and South Western Railway 'Baltic' tanks, although doing much good work, did not have the same attention as if their designer had still been in office at Kilmarnock. Furthermore, the policy of the L.M.S.R. was one of standardization, and a small class of 6 locomotives was doomed to early extinction. Nevertheless they were fine engines, and in other circumstances would no doubt have had a distinguished career.

149 Metropolitan Railway; Charles Jones's 4-4-4 express tank engine.

Beginning with the purely Underground section from Bishops Road to Farringdon Street, opened in 1863, the Metropolitan

Railway extended far out beyond the northern suburbs of London, to Aylesbury, and Verney Junction through a delightful part of the Chiltern Hills, in Buckinghamshire. Claiming it for themselves the railway exhorted town-dwellers to live in 'Metroland', and a number of very attractive services were run from Verney Junction, Aylesbury, and Chesham to the City. Luxurious bogie coaches were introduced and some trains even had a Pullman car. They were electrically hauled as far as Harrow-on-the-Hill, and then there was a change-over to steam. Some smart running was required on these popular residential trains, and after a trial of 0-6-4 tank engines, Jones introduced the handsome and efficient 4-4-4 tanks shown in our picture. These engines had to run fast, but were also required to climb well, because the line north of Rickmansworth mounts into the Chiltern Hills on a continuous gradient of 1 in 100. Though there was much express running on the London side of Rickmansworth, beyond that point the Metropolitan trains called at all stations, and hard work was involved in getting away from Chorley Wood, and Chalfont Road, against the continuous rising gradient. These engines did the job most competently.

150 J. G. Robinson's Historic 2-8-0.

Although passenger traffic on the London Extension never developed to the extent hoped for, in the north the freight and mineral traffic of the Great Central Railway was enormous. In 1911 Robinson built the first of a new design of large 2-8-0, and it was put through extensive trials. Proving thoroughly successful, an order for no fewer than 70 engines was placed with the North British Locomotive Company, and delivery of these was taken in 1912–13. The Great Central eventually had 127 of these tough, hard-working engines, but during World War I the design was chosen for general service on

military railways abroad, and a total of 521 were built by various firms for service with the Railway Operating Division of the British Army. Our picture shows one of these engines fitted with the Westinghouse brake, unlike the Great Central examples, which used the vacuum. After war service many of these R.O.D. engines were purchased by British railways other than the Great Central, and numbers of them were put to work on the London and North Western, the Caledonian, and the Great Western. On the last mentioned line they were so well liked as to become almost a G.W.R. standard type. After the grouping no fewer than 273 of them were acquired by the L.N.E.R., and used all over the system. This Robinson design must be set down as one of the most successful heavy freight engines of all time.

151 A Great Western 'Castle'.

It is no exaggeration to state that the 'Castle' is one of the most famous and successful locomotive designs the world has ever seen. Engines of this class, to an unchanged design, were built at intervals from 1923 to 1939, and after the end of World War II construction continued, to a design modified only to the extent of a different superheater, and altered arrangements for lubrication, until 1950, by which time no fewer than 171 were running. They were a development of the Churchward 'Star' class, and included all the virtues of the latter, plus the advantages of improved manufacturing techniques at Swindon, and precision methods in repair. Fast and economical in service, many notable records were claimed by the 'Castle' locomotives, including the fastest-ever start-to-stop run from Swindon to Paddington by the Cheltenham Flyer in 1932: 77.3 miles at an average speed of 81.6 m.p.h. with the *Tregenna Castle*; a run non-stop to Plymouth in 1925 with the *Caldicot Castle* and with the maximum load of the

Cornish Riviera Express when the arrival at North Road was 15 min. early, and a maximum speed of 100 m.p.h. down the Honeybourne bank by the *Builth Castle*. The pioneer engine, No. 4073 *Caerphilly Castle* is now in the Science Museum, South Kensington.

152 Lancashire and Yorkshire Railway; 'Class 8' 4-cylinder 4-6-0

In 1908 George Hughes had put on the road a class of non-superheated four-cylinder 4-6-0 locomotives of huge and impressive appearance. They were intended for rapid acceleration and heavy work on the main lines; but it is perhaps no exaggeration to say that gradually they gained a reputation for being 'the world's worst'. In 1920 a most intensive rebuilding was carried out, including a redesigned front-end, and the adding of a superheater. The engines were transformed and did excellent work. They had scarcely got into their stride when the grouping of the railways came in 1923, and their designer George Hughes was appointed Chief Mechanical Engineer of the L.M.S.R. In addition to the rebuilding of all the original L.&Y.R. engines of 1908, another 55 were built between 1921 and 1925. Many of them were allocated to working on the northern section of the former London and North Western Railway where they did good work over Shap. Always masters of their work they were nevertheless very heavy coal burners, and in comparative trials with various locomotives, in 1925, they proved considerably less economical than the London and North Western 'Claughton' class, with which they were classified on equality so far as loading was concerned. Our picture shows one of the original engines of 1908, as rebuilt. Later, all the class were painted in 'Derby red'.

153 The First Gresley Pacific; G.N.R.

It is no exaggeration to say that the building of the two prototype 'Pacific' engines Nos. 1470 and 1471 at Doncaster Works in 1922 marked the beginning of a new locomotive era in Great Britain. Although an experimental Pacific had been built by the Great Western Railway as long previously as 1908 that engine, No. 111 *The Great Bear*, had been an isolated unit, and formed no part of the standard pattern of locomotive operating on the G.W.R. On the other hand the Great Northern 'Pacifics' were destined to become an L.N.E.R. standard for all important express train working between London and Edinburgh, and with their success and ever increasing prowess the term 'big engine' took on a new meaning in the nineteen-twenties. But to revert to their first introduction, in size and tractive power they represented just as great an advance over the Ivatt 'Atlantics' as the latter engines did over the Stirling eight-foot 'singles'. Yet revolutionary though they were in size they represented an entirely logical step in the development, and their design was entirely in the Doncaster tradition. In the case of so great an advance in size it could hardly be expected that finality in design would be achieved at once. After some years alterations to the valve gear were found desirable. But from 1927 onwards after these changes had been made, the design, in its performance no less than its bold conception, became one of the classics of British steam locomotive history.

154 Sir Vincent Raven's Pacific.

The North Eastern Railway had a very long tradition of excellent and individualistic locomotive design, and just before the railway itself became merged into the L.N.E.R. group, the last Chief Mechanical Engineer, Sir Vincent Raven, produced the first of his huge Pacifics. These engines, of which five were built at Darlington Works, were a natural development from the very successful three-cylinder Atlantics of Class 'Z'. In this respect they were unlike the contemporary 'Pacifics' of Sir Nigel Gresley, on the Great Northern. The latter represented an entirely new concept in design from Doncaster works rather than a straight enlargement of the previous 'Atlantic' engines. The Raven Pacifics were a pure enlargement in boiler and length, and in the perpetuation of the use of three sets of Stephenson link motion for actuating the valves. When Gresley was appointed Chief Mechanical Engineer of the L.N.E.R. he had to decide which 'Pacific' design to adopt as a future standard. Other things being equal he would naturally be inclined to favour his own design; but in trials with the dynamometer car between Doncaster and Kings Cross in 1923 the Great Northern engine showed a definite superiority over her North Eastern rival. Nevertheless the N.E.R. did some excellent work, and as the final expression of North Eastern design practice these Raven 'Pacifics' occupy a notable place in locomotive history.

155 The 'King Arthur' Class; Southern Railway.

This famous class of locomotives, one of the most generally successful of any during the Grouping Era of 1923–48, had its origin on the London and South Western Railway in 1918, when R. W. Urie built the first of 20 very powerful two-cylinder 4-6-os. They were designed in what might be termed the Eastleigh-Scottish tradition of massive frame design, and complete immunity from running troubles. In heavy express service however their performance left a little to be desired, and after grouping R. E. L. Maunsell and his staff made a number of small, but highly important modifications. The draughting was altered; there were changes to the valve gear, and the boiler pressure was raised. The result was to produce a masterpiece. Many of these engines were built subsequently for general use on the Southern Railway. The example illus-

trated, No. 768 *Sir Balin* was originally a boat train engine working between Victoria and Dover. Then it was transferred to the West of England, and earned a fine reputation on the heavy road between Salisbury and Exeter, while since nationalization it has been back at its original station, Stewarts Lane, Battersea, for working Kent Coast trains. Our picture shows the six-wheeled tender fitted to a number of these engines when engaged on services such as the Brighton and Ramsgate lines where the length of turntable at one time precluded use of the standard bogie tender.

156 An L.M.S. Standard Compound.

Following the finalization of the Midland superheated compound design (reference 110), and its very successful performances in tests against other locomotives of comparable power within the L.M.S. group, certain modifications were made to the design to make it suitable as an L.M.S. standard. In the first post-grouping batches trials were made with slightly enlarged cylinders, and a reversion to the original valve setting. But further comparative trials over the very severe main line between Leeds and Carlisle confirmed the dimensions as established on the Midland Railway as most suitable, except that the coupled wheels were 6 ft. 9 in. instead of 7 ft. in diameter, and that the appearance of the engines was somewhat changed by the need to use shorter chimneys and dome covers to suit the reduced height of the loading gauge in Scotland. The driver's position was changed from the right-hand to the left-hand side of the cab. As thus standardized, the three-cylindered compounds did many years of splendid work. Especially fine was their performance on the heavily graded routes of the Scottish Border country. There were 190 in all of the 'standard' compounds, and they worked as far afield as Aberdeen, Stranraer, York, Holyhead, Lincoln, and Bristol, in addition of course to running the principal main lines from London.

157 An L.M.S. Standard Goods.
The Midland Railway, in pre-grouping days, had one of the heaviest coal and mineral traffics in Great Britain. As in passenger working, the company favoured the use of locomotives of moderate power, and although some powerful 2-8-os were built at Derby for the Somerset and Dorset Joint Line the Fowler superheater 0-6-0 of 1911 was the largest freight locomotive built for purely Midland Railway usage. These very simple and economical engines were cheap to build and cheap to run, and 191 of them were built prior to the grouping. The general usefulness of the class led to its being adopted as an L.M.S.R. standard, and the engine illustrated is one of 580 built for general use all over the L.M.S. system from 1924 onward. It differs from the Midland design of 1911 only in having reduced height chimney and dome. The relatively large diameter of the coupled wheels, namely 5 ft. 3 in., enabled these engines to show a good turn of speed when required, and in consequence they were frequently called upon for passenger work on branch and secondary routes. On the Highland section, on the Somerset and Dorset, and on the Furness line they were often used on passenger trains. Five of them were built new for the Somerset and Dorset in 1922. While they were naturally not up to main line express passenger service they could otherwise be described as maids of all work.

158 The 'Sandringham' Class 4-6-0;
London and North Eastern Railway.
After the grouping of the railways, in 1923, the loading of express trains in many parts of the country was very much on the increase due to the use of more luxurious stock, the introduction of additional amenities, and so on. While this could be met on the trunk lines to the north by building larger and more powerful locomotives it could not be done in East Anglia. Over the lines of the former Great Eastern Railway restrictions did not only apply to axle loading and clearances. The turntables set a limit upon the overall length unless a cumbersome process of uncoupling engine from tender was to be followed. To provide enhanced power within the existing civil engineering restrictions Gresley introduced the 'Sandringham' class, in 1928. By use of three cylinders a better arrangement of balancing was obtained, thereby permitting a heavier dead weight per axle, than with a two-cylinder machine having the same amount of balance of the reciprocating parts. The 'Sandringhams', of which the first examples were named after country houses and estates in East Anglia, were very successful. Many additional engines of the class were built subsequently for the Great Central line, and as the latter railway did not suffer from turntable restrictions it was possible to fit larger tenders. The engines allocated to the Great Central line were mostly named after well-known football clubs. They were very fast and economical machines and frequently attained speeds of 90 m.p.h. In all, 73 of them were constructed.

159 The 'Lord Nelson'; Southern Railway.
While the 'King Arthur' class 4-6-os were capable of excellent work they were no more than medium-powered engines by the standards of the mid-nineteen-twenties, and when the Traffic Manager of the Southern Railway announced his intention of running express trains of 500 tons weight at average speeds of 55 m.p.h. it was evident that locomotives of considerably enhanced power would be necessary. Maunsell and his staff carried out the most careful investigations before deciding on the main features of the new design. With the assistance of the Great

Western and of the London and North Eastern Railways James Clayton personally studied the working of the 'Castle' class 4-6-os, and of the first Gresley 'Pacifics', and eventually a four-cylinder 4-6-o was decided upon. Its unusual feature was the setting of the cranks at 135 deg., giving eight exhausts per revolution, instead of the usual four. Named after great Naval commanders, the 'Lord Nelson' class proved very fast and powerful engines, though they needed greater skill and experience in driving and firing than the general utility, workaday 'King Arthurs'. After he succeeded Maunsell as Chief Mechanical Engineer of the railway, O. V. S. Bulleid improved the 'Nelsons' by fitting multiple jet blastpipes and an improved design of cylinders. Our picture shows the 'Lord Nelson' as originally built in 1926.

160 The 'Royal Scot' Class 4-6-o; L.M.S.R.

Rarely can a famous locomotive design have been evolved in more curious and roundabout circumstances than the 'Royal Scot'. Sir Henry Fowler was planning a 4-cylinder compound 'Pacific', while other influences on the L.M.S.R. considered that a 4-6-o was large enough for all requirements. In the autumn of 1926 a 'Castle' class 4-6-o was borrowed from the Great Western and tested between Euston and Carlisle, with the result that a decision was taken to have 50 3-cylinder 4-6-os built at top speed by the North British Locomotive Company. So urgently were the new engines needed that in Glasgow the order was divided between the Hyde Park and the Queens Park Works of the manufacturer – 25 apiece. The 'Scots' were an immediate success, and did a great deal of very hard work between Euston and Glasgow. Originally, half of them were named after Scottish regiments – a gesture by the L.M.S.R. that created much interest and satisfaction in Scotland; the remainder

were named after historic locomotives ranging from the *Lancashire Witch* to the *Lady of the Lake*. The 'Scots' were much improved in detail by Sir William Stanier, who incorporated some important features of Great Western practice after his arrival on the L.M.S.R. in 1932; and between that time and the outbreak of World War II these engines were among the most effective express passenger 4-6-os in the country.

161 The 'King George V'.

The 'King' class, which represents the ultimate development of the historic Churchward four-cylinder 4-6-o design, had the greatest nominal tractive effort of any British 4-6-o express locomotive, and was in fact equal in this respect to the much larger and heavier Pacific locomotives of the other British railways. The 'Kings', apart from the technical features of the design that made such a tremendous concentration of power possible, had several other great distinctions. The first engine of the class, No. 6000 *King George V*, virtually made its *début* in the U.S.A. For after a very short period of 'running in' it was shipped to America to represent Great Britain at the Centenary celebrations of the Baltimore and Ohio Railroad; and while in the U.S.A. the engine did some very notable work. At home the introduction of the 'Kings' made possible some accelerations of the West of England services, despite ever-increasing loads, and the thirty engines of this class spent the entire 32–35 years of their lives in the heaviest express passenger traffic. No. 6000 *King George V* is now preserved, and will be housed in the Great Western Railway Museum at Swindon.

162 The Gresley Super-Pacific; L.N.E.R.

The original Great Northern 'Pacifics' were designed in the Doncaster tradition of old, and had a boiler pressure of 180 lb.

per sq. in. As a result of the Interchange Trials with the Great Western Railway in 1925, when a 'Castle' class 4-6-0 carrying a pressure of 225 lb. per sq. in. proved the more economical, Gresley began experimenting with higher boiler pressures on his 'Pacifics', and of two trial engines one, No. 2544 *Lemberg*, had its cylinders reduced in diameter so that its nominal tractive effort, using 220 lb. per sq. in., was the same as that of the standard 180 lb. engines. A series of trials with the dynamometer car was run between Doncaster and Kings Cross, running *Lemberg* against a standard engines No. 4473 *Solario*. Taken all round there was very little in it, but Gresley was sufficiently impressed with the work of *Lemberg* to make 220 lb. per sq. in. his new standard for 'Pacific' engines, and in a new series, built at Doncaster in 1930, he used cylinders slightly larger than those of the experimental *Lemberg*. The new series, known as Class 'A3' thus had a higher tractive effort than the original Gresley 'Pacifics'. They proved very fast, powerful, and economical engines, and in 1935 No. 2750 *Papyrus*, in the course of a trial run from London to Newcastle and back, broke many world records for steam traction including the attainment of a maximum speed of 108 m.p.h. In due course, as the boilers became due for renewal, all the original 180 lb. Pacifics were converted to Class 'A3'.

163 An L.M.S. Horwich Mogul.

After the grouping of the railways in 1923, George Hughes of the former Lancashire and Yorkshire Railway was appointed Chief Mechanical Engineer of the L.M.S.R., and his former head-quarters at Horwich, Lancashire, became H.Q. for the entire L.M.S.R. for a time. A general service locomotive, capable of taking fast goods or intermediate passenger trains was urgently needed, and the powerful 2-6-0 illustrated in our pic-

ture was designed and the first examples built at Horwich. To accommodate the very large cylinders outside they had to be located high up, and inclined at quite a steep angle. This feature, together with the working of the outside valve gear, led to these engines being nicknamed the 'Crabs'. When first introduced they were finished in the passenger livery of 'Derby red'; but our picture shows them in the guise familiar in later years. Despite their relatively small coupled wheels they were free running, and frequently attained speeds of 75 m.p.h. But they were at their best in hard slogging with heavy freight trains, or in working passenger trains on heavily graded routes. Some of them were used with success on the Highland line in Scotland, and they were much in demand for excursions, football specials, and suchlike traffic.

164 The G.W.R. 'Hall' Class.

During the nineteen-twenties 4-6-0 locomotives with four cylinders were standardized for express passenger work on the G.W.R., and to the 73 engines of the 'Star' class were added many new 'Castles' and the very powerful 'Kings'. But the two-cylinder 4-6-0s of the 'Saint' class, fitted with Churchward's very effective setting of the Stephenson link motion, were exceptionally smart in getting away from rest, and in C. B. Collett's time it was decided to use this engine design for an intermediate passenger and fast mixed traffic engine. An experiment was made by rebuilding engine No. 2925 *Saint Martin* with 6 ft. wheels, instead of the original 6 ft. 8½ in.; and the rebuilt engine did so well that she became the prototype of a new and ultimately very numerous class, named after country estates. So many of these engines were built eventually that the list of 'stately homes' in Great Western territory became completely exhausted, and some of the later engines of the class had names taken from as far afield as

Lancashire, the Lake District, and the East Riding of Yorkshire. In all, 330 of these engines were built. They were extremely fast runners, having regard to their wheel diameter, and on one occasion, in emergency, one of them ran the Bristolian, more than keeping the very fast sectional times then scheduled. The engine illustrated, No. 5930 *Hannington Hall* was one of a series built before the war.

165 Gresley's 'Shire' Class 4-4-0.

In building standard locomotives for use on many different sections of the L.N.E.R. Gresley used three-cylinder propulsion, with the conjugated valve motion that he had developed on the Great Northern Railway prior to grouping. The 'D49' was an interesting example of the application of a 3-cylinder layout to a large modern 4-4-0. The first engines of the class, designated D49/1 were built in 1927, and had piston valves, Walschearts gear, and the Gresley conjugated motion, for the middle cylinders. This series was named after counties served by the L.N.E.R., as in the case of the engine shown in our picture, No. 2754 *Rutlandshire*. A later series built in 1928, had Lentz rotary cam poppet valves. These latter were named after famous hunts in L.N.E.R. territory, and bore the figure of a fox in full flight above the nameplate. The 'Shires' were mostly used in Scotland, while the 'Hunts' were used around Leeds, Hull, York and Newcastle. Although slender in appearance, by reason of their high-pitched boiler, they were capable of hard work, though they tended to get rough in operation after their mileage after shopping had substantially increased. The poppet-valve engines were fast and free runners, and one of their regular turns for many years was the working of the morning express from Leeds to Scotland, which they took as far as Newcastle. This involved a fast non-stop run of 80 miles from York to New-

castle, which was often done at an average speed of nearly 60 m.p.h. from start to stop. Taking piston valve and poppet valve engines together the 'D49' class totalled 76 locomotives.

166 A Beyer-Garratt 2-6-0 + 0-6-2; L.M.S.R.

One of the great problems of modern railway operating has been to provide locomotives of adequate power without exceeding the limit of weight or length that can be permitted by the civil engineer. An easy, though uneconomical way of providing increased tractive power is to use two engines, though this also doubles the cost of working by having a second crew. The Beyer-Garratt type of locomotive, that has been used overseas in many countries of the British Commonwealth, consists virtually of two separate engines fed with steam from one very large central boiler. Thus two engines can be managed by one crew, though it needs some very heavy stoking to provide the necessary steam. On many engines of the Beyer-Garratt type mechanical stokers are fitted. The L.M.S.R. example illustrated provides the equivalent of two standard 2-6-0 engines (reference 163). These enormous engines were used on the very heavy coal traffic of the former Midland Railway between Toton marshalling yards, near Nottingham, and the London distributional yards for the coal trade, at Cricklewood. It was a long, slow haul, and the Beyer-Garratts put in many years of good service on the job.

167 L.M.S. '5XP' (Baby Scot).

After grouping a sustained attempt was made by the L.M.S.R. to develop a locomotive of enhanced power from the L.N.W.R. 'Claughton' class. Considerable success attended the fitting of enlarged boilers on to a number of the ex-L.N.W.R. locomotives. But the success of the 3-cylinder 'Royal Scots' suggested that a more extensive reconstruction might prove profitable, and a new design was worked out using a synthesis of standard parts. This consisted of a 3-cylinder front-end and motion, on the lines of the 'Royal Scots', but using the enlarged 'Claughton' boiler. The result was a handsome and successful locomotive, strongly reminiscent of the 'Royal Scot' in external style, but with a smaller boiler. The resemblance suggested the original nickname of 'Baby Scots'. At a slightly later time the scrapping of the famous London and North Western war memorial engine *Patriot* led to the perpetuation of the name on a 'Baby Scot', together with the inscription that accompanied the name, and from that time the engines were known as the 'Patriot' class. Eventually the class was 52 strong. They were fast and powerful engines. Some retained the name of the L.N.W.R. 'Claughtons' they replaced; others were unnamed, and a few had names with special associations such as the engine illustrated No. 5538, which was named after Giggleswick School, lying within sight of the Anglo-Scottish main line of the Midland Division, over which this engine regularly worked.

168   A Southern 'School'.

Locomotives of enhanced power were required in 1930 for the Hastings line of the former S.E.&C. Railway. It is a most awkward route, with heavy gradients, much curvature, and serious engineering restrictions in the clearances available in the tunnels just south of Tunbridge Wells. Maunsell would like to have used the 'King Arthur' 4-6-0s, but the clearances and weight restrictions prevented this being done. A new design had to be worked out, as quickly and cheaply as possible. The result was once aptly described as a 'three-quarter Nelson'! The cylinders and valve gear were the same as the 'Nelson', but using three instead of four, but the boiler was a shortened version of that fitted to the

'King Arthur'. The 'School' was thus a synthesis of detail made up very economically from existing patterns and tools. No synthesis – a virtual makeshift! – can have been more outstandingly successful. Far from being a special type confined to the difficult conditions of the Hastings line, the 'Schools' came to do magnificent work on the fast Portsmouth trains, and eventually they superseded the 'King Arthurs' on the Bournemouth expresses. They were light on coal, and could tackle loads of 450 tons as a matter of course. They were, without any doubt, the most successful 4-4-0 locomotives ever to run in Great Britain. The engine *Stowe* of this class has been preserved, and is contained in Lord Montagu of Beaulieu's Motor Museum, at Beaulieu, Hampshire.

169   A Pannier Tank; Great Western Railway.

The Great Western was always a very large user of tank engines, and from its own diverse early designs, and from the large variety of engines that came into the stock from the local railways in South Wales after the amalgamation of 1923, it owned at one time more than 1,000 of the 0-6-0 type alone. In 1929, from the famous Dean 0-6-0 tender engine (reference 45), there was designed a modern tank engine that could be standardized and built in large numbers to replace the diversity of older engines that existed. Except that the tank engine did not have a superheater the boiler and firebox were the same as those of the Dean goods, and the cylinders and motion were the same. The tank engines had 4 ft. 7½ in. coupled wheels, against 5 ft. 2 in. on the tender engine. The so-called '5700' class was a great success, and no fewer than 790 have been built since 1929. Though officially designated 'light goods and shunting engines', many of them were regularly used on passenger trains, and speeds of up to 65 m.p.h. have been recorded with them. The example shown in our picture is one of the series fitted with condensing apparatus for working the meat trains through the Metropolitan line tunnels to Smithfield Market. As dieselization spread over the Western Region of British Railways, and many of these engines became redundant, some were transferred to the Southern. A number of them did good work on the empty stock trains into and out of Waterloo, while a batch of them went to Folkestone Junction for working boat trains on the very sharp incline between the Junction and the Harbour station.

170 A Stanier 'Black Five'; L.M.S.

If a competition were to be held for the most generally useful locomotive class ever to run on British metals the Stanier 'Black-Five' would be a very strong candidate for the prize. In principle the idea of a general-utility 4-6-0 of inter-mediate power capacity, and of such dimensions as to be usable over almost the entire mileage of the L.M.S.R., undoubtedly stemmed from the success of the Great Western 'Hall' class (reference 164). But the Stanier Class 5, 4-6-0, combining the best of both Great Western and L.M.S. practice, proved a remarkable engine, able to take heavy and fast express passenger trains on virtually equal terms with the 'Royal Scots' (reference 160), do heavy goods work, and run up to 90 m.p.h. on the moderate-loaded express trains of the Midland line. As mixed traffic units they were painted black, hence their unofficial designation of 'Black-Fives'. They were used all over the L.M.S.R. system, from Bournemouth to Wick, from Swansea to York, and were universally acclaimed. The design was first introduced in 1934, and at first it was not finalized. The first 70 engines were subject to modification; but from 1935 onwards they were built in large numbers, down to the year 1951. Ultimately there were 842 of the class in service.

171 A Gresley 'P2'; L.N.E.R.

Sir Nigel Gresley, as a true successor to Stirling and Ivatt, in the locomotive 'chair' of the Great Northern Railway, at Doncaster, greatly disliked double-heading. The old Doncaster tradition of 'one train, one engine' persisted with him, and when faced with a serious haulage problem on the East Coast Route north of Edinburgh, where even his Pacifics could not take the heaviest trains, he designed the mighty 'P2' class, of 2-8-2s. These were 3-cylinder machines, with 6 ft. 2 in. coupled wheels, and an enormous boiler. The first two engines of the class had an arrangement of smoke-deflecting screens at the front-end, but the later ones had the same streamlined 'prow' as proved so successful on the high speed 'A4' Pacifics. The 'P2' class, of which six were built specially for service between Edinburgh and Aberdeen, were very successful as weight pullers. While the Reid 'Atlantics' were limited to 340 tons, tare, and the 'Pacific' to 450 tons, the 'P2' class took 550 tons and more with equal success. Unfortunately the conditions that developed during World War II led to their maintenance deteriorating, with consequent troubles and failures; and after Gresley's death they were rebuilt as 4-6-2s, and became less effective. In their prime, however, they ranked as the most powerful engines ever to run in this country.

172 A World Record Breaker; Gresley's *Mallard*, Class 'A4'.

These world-famous engines represented the consummation of the story of Pacific locomotive development at Doncaster. Into them Gresley put those finishing touches to the already very successful 'A3', in the form of still higher boiler pressure, larger diameter piston valves, and the internal streamlining of steam ports and passages. These features substantially improved the haulage capacity and speedworthiness of the engines, while the very striking form of the external streamlining fairly captured popular imagination. The first four engines were designed for the Silver Jubilee high speed service, and were finished in silver, and when the pioneer engine, No. 2509 *Silver Link* attained a maximum speed of 112 m.p.h. on its very first public trip the fame of the class was assured from the outset. From this spectacular beginning the 'A4s' have gone from strength to strength. They hauled tremendous loads at ordinary express speeds; they frequently topped 100 m.p.h. in ordinary service, and in 1938 engine No. 4468 *Mallard* made the world record for steam traction with a maximum speed of 126 m.p.h. After the first four 'silver' engines garter blue became the standard colour for the class, in L.N.E.R. days. Down to the year 1962 they remained in first class express service, one of the finest of their latter-day achievements being the haulage each summer of the Elizabethan express, non-stop over the $392\frac{3}{4}$ miles between Kings Cross and Edinburgh, in $6\frac{1}{2}$ hours, an average speed of $60\frac{1}{2}$ m.p.h. over this long distance with a normal load of about 420 tons.

173 The 'Princess Elizabeth'; L.M.S.R.

After Sir William Stanier had taken up his appointment as Chief Mechanical Engineer of the L.M.S.R. designs were put in hand for new express locomotives that could work the Anglo-Scottish expresses through between London and Glasgow, 401 miles. Hitherto the longest working undertaken by a single locomotive on the L.M.S.R. had been the 299-mile run between London and Carlisle. Stanier embodied the fruits of his long experience on the Great Western in a front-end design very similar to that of the G.W.R. 'King' class; but he put on a very much larger boiler and firebox and used the 'Pacific' wheel arrangement, 4-6-2. The first two engines of this new

class were completed at Crewe in 1933 and named *The Princess Royal* and *Princess Elizabeth*. It was from this latter name that the class derived its affectionate nickname of the 'Lizzies'. After some experimental running, and subsequent modifications to the boilers, the 'Lizzies' became a great success, and did that which was expected of them in long-distance running. To the *Princess Elizabeth* belongs the credit of one of the greatest runs in British railway history, in November 1936, when a special train of 260 tons was worked non-stop from Glasgow to Euston at an average speed throughout of 70 m.p.h. – $401\frac{1}{4}$ miles in $344\frac{3}{4}$ min. start to stop.

174 The 'Coronation' of 1937; L.M.S.

To celebrate the Coronation of His Majesty King George VI in 1937, the L.M.S.R. put on a new express between London and Glasgow, 'The Coronation Scot', making the $401\frac{1}{4}$ mile run in $6\frac{1}{2}$ hours, inclusive of a stop at Carlisle. From the experience with the 'Princess Royal' class 4-6-2s it seemed that considerable improvements could be made in a 'Pacific' locomotive designed expressly for continuous running at high speed; at the same time such improvements in performance as seemed possible would also be of great benefit in the working of the ordinary expresses of the line, many of which it was desired to accelerate. The five new engines built specially for the 'Coronation Scot' service were finished in Prussian Blue, and the streamlined form was designed to minimize air resistance at high speed. These engines gave remarkable results. On a trial trip before the 'Coronation Scot' service was inaugurated a speed of 114 m.p.h. was attained, and the return run from Crewe to Euston, 158 miles, made in 119 minutes – an average speed of 79.7 m.p.h. A later engine of the class, streamlined, but finished in the standard L.M.S. red livery did some notable running on American railroads in 1939, when it was exhibited at the New York World's Fair in that year. The engine that thus crossed the Atlantic was actually named *Coronation*, but the name was transferred from the first of the blue engines of 1937 specially for this visit to America.

175 A 'Green Arrow'; London and North Eastern Railway.

The Great Northern Railway was a pioneer in the practice of running fast goods trains, carrying block loads, with all vehicles fitted with continuous automatic vacuum brake, and with scheduled speeds of about 45 m.p.h., start to stop, over runs such as from London to Peterborough, Peterborough to York and so on, powerful locomotives were needed when these trains were loaded to 40 and 50 wagons. In early L.N.E.R. days the 'K3' type 2-6-0s were used, but Gresley felt that there was scope for a still more powerful class and in 1936 he brought out the first of the 'V2s', No. 4771 *Green Arrow*. It had a shortened version of the standard 'Pacific' boiler, and a leading pony truck like that of the 'K3'. Four engines were built for trial, but such was their success and versatility that when quantity production of the class began they came to be regarded as reserve express passenger engines, and on top form there was little difference between their finest work and that of the 'A3' express passenger 'Pacifics'. In heavy goods service they could tackle anything the traffic department liked to hang on behind them. In passenger service, before World War II, they occasionally deputized for the streamlined 'A4' Pacifics on the high-speed limited trains. In ordinary express service they frequently attained speeds of 90 m.p.h. They were particularly successful in the moderate-speed heavily-loaded passenger traffic of war time. In all 184 of them were built.

176 A Stanier '8F'.

This excellent design formed the heavy-freight equivalent of the Stanier 'Black-Five' (reference 170), but used more particularly in general goods service. The design was introduced on the L.M.S.R. in 1935, but the need for new freight engines was not so great as for passenger and mixed traffic units, and by the outbreak of war in September 1939 only 126 of them had been built. Then orders were placed by the Government for 240 of them for overseas service. They were equipped for oil burning, and did much good work in Egypt, Palestine, Iraq, and Persia. Then, as the war effort at home intensified, and more locomotives were needed for freight traffic, this Stanier design was selected for production as a national standard, and engines of this type were eventually being built at Ashford, Brighton, Darlington, Doncaster, Eastleigh and Swindon, in addition to many more in the various works of the L.M.S.R. At its maximum strength the class, as running on British Railways, numbered 719 strong, including many that were returned to Great Britain after war service overseas. Although primarily a goods engine the '8F' has a fine turn of speed, and when used in emergency on passenger trains they have been known to exceed 60 m.p.h.

177 An L.M.S. 'Jubilee'.

In providing a stud of new standard locomotives for the L.M.S.R. Sir William Stanier built, simultaneously, 4-6-0s for both mixed traffic, and for purely express passenger duties. The mixed traffic units were the very celebrated 'Black-Fives' (reference 170), while for express passenger service he built a 3-cylinder engine, of capacity roughly equal to that of the 'Baby Scots' (reference 167), but with taper boilers. Although more expensive to construct, the taper boilers amply paid off their prime cost by being much lighter on maintenance costs, and less subject to incidental troubles. The new 3-cylinder 4-6-0s were at first unnamed, but in 1935, in honour of the Silver Jubilee of His Majesty King George V, one of them, No. 5552, was specially named *Silver Jubilee*, and many others of the class were named after units of the British Commonwealth. The 'Jubilees', as the class became known, were built to a total of 190 engines. After some slight teething troubles they became first-class motive power units, and worked over most of the L.M.S.R. main lines. Although they were extremely fast engines they seemed to excel at high speed climbing of the banks on the Midland route to Scotland, and some fine records of their performance were obtained on the severe route between Leeds and Carlisle. Originally they were finished in 'Derby red'; but since nationalization they have been painted in the standard British Railways green.

178 'Sir William A. Stanier F.R.S.'; L.M.S.

The first Stanier Pacifics were built at Crewe in 1933 (reference 173) and these were followed four years later by the streamlined 'Coronations'. Although a number of streamlined 'Pacifics' were added to the stock it was found that the additional cost and weight of the streamlined casing was not really justified, and newer locomotives of the class were built without it. Furthermore the casings were in time removed from the earlier engines. In post-war years a number of aids to improved performance were added to these engines, such as self-cleaning smokeboxes, hopper ashpans, rocking firegrates, and roller bearings on all axles; and in many respects the last two locomotives of this class, built in 1947, represent the highest development of the British express passenger steam locomotive. It is therefore appropriate that one of these should be named after so great a steam locomotive engineer as Sir William Stanier. The engine is shown here in the post-war standard livery of the L.M.S.R., black with maroon edging; but since nationalization these engines have borne many colours, from the experimental 'blues' to British Railways standard green, and finally a reversion to 'Derby red'. To one of these engines, the *Duchess of Gloucester*, belongs the honour of having attained the highest power output ever recorded with steam in a dynamometer car test in Great Britain.

179 The Vale of Rheidol Line; a Swindon-built tank engine.

The Vale of Rheidol narrow gauge line was originally an independent concern, but came within the Great Western system in 1923. Today it is the only part of British Railways to be built to a sub-standard rail gauge – only 1 ft. 11½ in. against the standard 4 ft. 8½ in. The journey from Aberystwyth to the Devil's Bridge is an enthralling one from the scenic point of view, but arduous work for the locomotive. The track winds incessantly, on very sharp curves, as it makes its way up the mountainside, and very careful work by both driver and fireman is needed to keep a full head of steam in such conditions. The gradient is 1 in 50 continuously. The smart little 2-6-2 tank engines were designed by the G.W.R. in 1923, specially for the job, and built at Swindon Works. Originally they were finished in plain green with the words GREAT WESTERN in large letters on their tank sides. Since nationalization, however, the engines concerned have all been named, and it is in this present form that one of them, *Owain Glyndwr*, is shown in our picture. It is interesting to find that the Welsh, rather than the English spelling of the name is used. A second engine of the class is named *Llywelyn*, and the third is the *Prince of Wales*. These little engines weigh no more than 25 tons in working order.

180 **Talyllyn Railway;** the original engine.

The Talyllyn Railway has a special place in the history of railways in Great Britain, as being the first to be rescued from closure and disappearance through the activities of a Preservation Society. It is only a tiny little line, 6.6 miles long from Towyn to Abergynolwyn; but the devoted activities of the Preservation Society have resulted not only in the preservation, but the restoration to fully working order of one of the original locomotives, No. 1 *Talyllyn*. This little engine, which weighs no more than 10 tons in working order, was built in 1865 by Fletcher, Jennings and Company of the Lowca Engine Works, Whitehaven. It runs on the 2 ft. 3 in. gauge used on some Welsh narrow gauge railways. When the Preservation Society took charge of things engine No. 1 was in a very run-down condition; but through the generosity of several members of the society she was fully repaired and restored, and in 1959 took the road once more in excellent condition. No speed records are made on the Talyllyn, however. A typical run up the valley, with a heavy train, takes about 55 min. including 10 to 15 min. standing at stations. But it is a district in which no one wishes to hurry, and it is pleasant to trundle along in an open carriage behind so ornate a 'period piece' of a locomotive.

181 **Isle of Man Railway;** a Beyer-Peacock tank engine.

In the Isle of Man railways were laid to the 3 ft. gauge, and from their first opening until the present time reliance has been placed upon tank engines of the 2-4-0 type. The engine shown in our picture is the only one now to retain the original type of boiler, and the characteristic bell-mouthed dome, with Salter valves on the top. The remaining engines of this same design have been rebuilt with boilers having round-topped domes.

Originally the engines of the Isle of Man Railway were smartly turned out in a bright green, with much polished brass and copper work, and all are named with local associations. In recent years the livery has been changed to a pleasing shade of brown-madder, still with the adornments of old, and today no stud of steam locomotives are more smartly maintained. Although they are relatively small, having coupled wheels of only 3 ft. 9 in. diameter, they tackle heavy loads of passengers in the holiday season, and with their gay style of painting and profusion of flashing brasswork they make an extremely pretty sight running through the glens, or climbing beside the sea on the northern branch of the line to Ramsey.

182 **Romney, Hythe and Dymchurch Railway;** express locomotive *Hercules*.

Locomotives built to the narrow gauge of 1 ft. 3 in. – roughly one quarter of the British standard gauge – were introduced in the years before World War I for miniature passenger-carrying railways in pleasure grounds, exhibitions, and so on. Their first application on a public railway came when the Ravenglass and Eskdale Railway – formerly of 3 ft gauge, and in Chancery (!) – was converted, during World War I, and two 15 in. gauge 'model' express locomotives were put to work. The Romney, Hythe and Dymchurch Railway was a much more ambitious venture, and every summer it conveys large numbers of holiday makers. Most of the locomotives are 'Pacifics' of a design that could be called a free adaptation of the famous Gresley non-streamlined 'Pacifics' of the L.N.E.R. But in addition to the 'Pacifics' there are two 4-8-2s, designed originally for mixed traffic duties, and for hauling the heavy trains of shingle that are worked from the beaches between New Romney and Dungeness. They are remarkably powerful little engines, and will haul a train of open coaches sufficient to convey at least 150 passengers. With such a load the speed will often rise to 30 m.p.h. Fortunately there are no gradients on the line. From Hythe right out to Dungeness the track is virtually level throughout.

183 'Merchant Navy' Class.

The appointment of Mr O. V. S. Bulleid as Chief Mechanical Engineer of the Southern Railway, was the signal for a strong revival in steam locomotive activity. For some years previously nearly all attention had been concentrated on the extension of the electrified system. In the new 'Pacific' design of 1941 many features were included to combat the gradually worsening conditions of railway operation. The boiler and firebox were designed to use low-grade fuel; extensive use of welding was made in the construction of both boiler and chassis, to reduce weight; and to minimize maintenance work on the running gear the valve gear was totally enclosed in an oil bath. The exterior casing was of striking form, and the final touch of novelty was provided by the Box-poc form of driving wheels. Our picture shows one of these engines as originally built, in the pre-war Southern livery of malachite green. Additional cowling had to be introduced at a later date for smoke deflection at the front end. These engines proved very fast and powerful, but unfortunately some of the innovations, and particularly the valve gear, were troublesome and expensive to maintain, and in recent years the air-smoothed casings have been removed, and a conventional Walschaerts valve gear fitted in place of the totally enclosed gear of special design. The general appearance of the engines today is similar to that of the rebuilt 'West Country' Pacific, illustrated on plate 190, though the engines themselves are slightly larger.

184 A Thompson 'B1' 4-6-0; L.N.E.R.

After the death of Sir Nigel Gresley, in 1941, the new Chief Mechanical Engineer, Edward Thompson, was faced with the need for new locomotives of a mixed traffic character in the middle of the war, with all the restrictions upon tool-making and workshop plant that then existed. The 'B1' 4-6-0 was a very clever synthesis of existing standard parts built into a new engine design of a general utility character. Thus the boiler and firebox was that of a 'Sandringham' class (reference 158); the cylinders those of the ex-G.N.R. 'K2' Mogul (reference 129), and the wheels those of the 'Green Arrow' 2-6-2 (reference 175). In producing a new engine design no major new tools were necessary. The 'B1' class was a great success from the outset, and more than 350 of them have been put into service. They were primarily intended for mixed traffic duties, but when in good trim they have proved capable of very fine express work. During the Interchange trials of 1948, made after Nationalization to test the locomotives of the former private companies against each other, a 'B1' was set to haul a very heavy express train on the Great Western line between Bristol and Exeter: 14 coach trains weighing 500 tons were taken at sustained speeds of 68–69 m.p.h. on level track – a wonderful performance for so relatively small an engine.

185 The Rebuilt 'Royal Scot.'

The original 'Royal Scots' (reference 160) were very good engines for their day. But they included the conventional design of parallel boiler, and straight-sided Belpaire firebox. When the time came for replacement of the original boilers a decision was taken to fit new boilers, having the tapered barrel and other features of detail design that had proved so free from trouble, and so efficient in steam raising on the smaller 4-6-0s of the L.M.S.R. At the same time a more extensive rebuild of the entire engine was undertaken, providing new cylinders and valves, with the same advanced features of design that had proved so successful on the 'Coronation' Pacifics of 1937. The changes made a considerable difference in the outward appearance of the engines, but they made a remarkable improvement in the performance, so much so that in 1948, when the nationalized British Railways conducted a series of test runs between locomotives of the former privately-owned companies, the 'Rebuilt Royal Scots' were able to compete on very nearly equal terms with 'Pacifics' from other railways, although the difference in weight between these 4-6-os and their competitors ranged from between 10 to 20 tons. Eventually all 70 engines of the 'Royal Scot' class were rebuilt in conformity with this most successful modernization.

186 Austerity 2-8-0 of 1942.
During World War II, when plans were being made for the liberation of the countries of Western Europe over-run by the enemy, designs for a general service locomotive were required. Standard British designs, such as the Stanier '8F' of the L.M.S.R. (reference 176), were based on peacetime practice and running conditions, and something more suited to the rough conditions of service in proximity to a battle-field or in countries recently liberated was specified. The design for a massive 2-8-0 was prepared by R. A. Riddles, Mechanical and Electrical Engineer, Scotland, L.M.S.R., but then attached to the Ministry of Supply as Deputy Director General of Royal Engineer Equipment. The first engine of the new design was completed by the North British Locomotive Company, in 1943, and no fewer than 733 returned to service on British Railways after the war. Although built in austerity conditions, for austerity service, these engines have since won golden opinions in ordinary freight service at home. The design features

built into them for the roughest of usage, have rendered them singularly trouble-free, and in many parts of the country they are regarded as the best heavy freight engines that have ever run.

187 The Peppercorn 'A1'; L.N.E.R.
Following the great success of the Gresley Pacifics on the L.N.E.R. in years before World War II it was to be expected that post-war development would be based on the same design. During the war years however some trouble was experienced in maintaining the Gresley conjugated valve gear, and post-war designs included three separate sets of motion – one for each of the three cylinders. Arthur H. Peppercorn developed the Gresley boiler, using a larger firebox, and with the modification to the front-end previously mentioned he produced an engine capable of very hard work on the line. The Peppercorn Pacifics were not called upon for such high speeds as those regularly run by the Gresleys in pre-war years, but several instances have been recorded of speeds over 100 m.p.h. A locomotive engineer in the North of England once summed up the characteristics of the Gresley and Peppercorn engines thus: 'The Gresley's are the real "greyhounds" of the stud; but if you have to take 600 tons on a dirty night give me a Peppercorn.' The latter engines first appeared in L.N.E.R. apple-green; but later they were finished in the standard British Railways green, in which guise the engine in our picture is shown.

188 A 'Britannia' Pacific.
As a result of the Interchange trials of 1948 the engineers of the Railway Executive of the British Transport Commission, under the direction of Mr R. A. Riddles, the member for mechanical and electrical engineering, designed a series of new standard locomotives embodying features shown to be most satisfactory in the performance of the former companies'

locomotives. The first of these new designs to appear was the Class 7MT 'Pacific'. To emphasize its national rather than regional character the first of these engines was named *Britannia*, while others have been named after famous locomotives of the past, and famous characters in British history, literature, and fiction. The engine illustrated, No. 70037 *Hereward the Wake*, was in regular service in East Anglia. The 'Britannia's' might, in other circumstances, have had as long and distinguished a career as many of their predecessors in British locomotive history. But the decision to supersede steam traction entirely was made in 1955, and replacement of the 'Britannia's' by diesel-electric locomotives began in 1958. During their short career on express work, in East Anglia, on the Western Region, on the Irish Mails, and on the Continental expresses of the Southern the 'Britannia's' did much excellent work, with economic use of fuel.

189 A 'BR5' Mixed Traffic 4-6-0.

On the grounds of general utility and proven excellence in service the Railway Executive would have been fully justified in adopting the Stanier 'Black-Five' as one of the national standard engines. But Riddles and his staff were most anxious to avoid any appearance of favouring one of the former railways in preference to the others, and the new 'BR5' 4-6-0, while closely similar to the Stanier in its boiler and motion was 'styled' like the 'Britannia's' and other new designs, and incorporated a number of new details. The 'BR5' class have proved splendid engines. They have been allocated to depots in many parts of Great Britain, and have been universally welcomed. On the Eastern section of the Southern Region, in particular, although designated 'mixed-traffic' they were used with outstanding success on express passenger services to the North Kent coast resorts. Although

an 'alien' design, so far as the men were concerned, they had the rare distinction of being preferred to their own and well-tried 'King Arthur' class (reference 155). When the latter engines were being scrapped some of their names were transferred to the new 'BR5' 4-6-0s. British Railways adopted the livery of the former London and North Western Railway for its intermediate and mixed traffic types, and the 'BR5' is here shown in the same painting style as former Crewe celebrities, like the 'Precursors', 'Prince of Wales' 4-6-0s, and 'Claughtons'.

190 A 'West Country' 4-6-2.

Following the introduction of the Bulleid 'Merchant Navy' class Pacifics, in 1941, the Southern Railway built a lighter version of the same design in 1945 of which the earlier batches were named after places in the West of England served by the Southern Railway. After 48 of these engines had been put into service the 'Battle of Britain' series followed, named after personalities, aerodromes, and units engaged in the Battle of Britain, in 1940. A final series, bringing the total for the class up to 110 locomotives, was named after a further West Country towns. Like the 'Merchant Navy' class these engines were capable of excellent work; but they suffered from the same defects, and commencing in 1957 a number of them were rebuilt, with conventional valve gear, and with the air-smoothed casing removed. Our illustration shows No. 34028 *Eddystone*, of the rebuilt series, and very massive imposing locomotives they now look. The change has greatly improved their reliability without lessening their capacity for hard work or very fast running. *Eddystone* is shown in the standard British Railways livery. In addition to working over all main lines of the Southern Region some of these engines have done excellent work on the very heavily graded route of the former

Somerset and Dorset Joint Line between Bath and Bournemouth. Of the 110 locomotives of the class a total of 41 have been rebuilt in the style shown in the illustration.

191   A 'BR4' Standard 2-6-0.

The range of new British standard steam locomotive design introduced from 1951 onwards included a 4-6-0 of Class 4 capacity, three varieties of 2-6-0, and three varieties of passenger tank engine all styled in a similar manner to the 'Britannia' and the 'BR5'. The engine chosen for illustration is the very successful Class 4 2-6-0, first introduced in 1953. While bearing an unmistakeable 'family likeness' to the 'BR5', the 4MT 2-6-0 has achieved an individuality of its own. With relatively small coupled wheels of only 5 ft. 3 in. diameter the nominal tractive effort is high in relation to the size of the engine. At the same time the excellent design of cylinders and valves has permitted of the free flow of steam, and made the engine very fast on the road. In earlier days a wheel of at least 6 ft. 6 in. diameter was considered essential for express work; but these small engines run freely up to 75 m.p.h., and form an interesting and impressive example of the last phase of steam locomotive design in this country.

192   The 'Evening Star'.

The last of the standard steam locomotives introduced by R. A. Riddles was in every way the most remarkable and successful of all. There was need for a heavy freight engine having an ability to run on as many routes in the country as possible; and the decision was taken to use a boiler similar to that of the 'Britannia' and the 2-10-0 wheel arrangement. As fast, as well as heavy mineral service was envisaged the coupled wheels were made 5 ft. in diameter. The result was an extraordinary versatile and successful locomotive, of which more than 200 have been built. The versatility of the type does indeed stand as a tribute to the accumulated experience of more than 100 years in locomotive designing in this country, and as a fitting climax to the story. Although primarily intended for heavy goods service these engines are occasionally used on fast passenger trains, and one of them ran at *ninety miles per hour* with the 'Flying Scotsman'. It is fitting that the very last steam locomotive built for service on British Railways should have been to this outstanding design. While the rest of the class are painted plain black, without any lining, the last one, which was built at Swindon, was decked in the 'passenger green' and named *Evening Star*. It was put into service in 1960.

WHEEL ARRANGEMENTS

The Classification of locomotive types:

What is known as the Whyte system provides the most generally accepted method of classifying the various wheel arrangements of steam locomotives. This specifies the number of wheels in the groups of 'carrying' and driving wheels. Thus a locomotive with a leading four-wheeled bogie, six-coupled driving wheels, and no carrying wheels at the trailing end is a 4-6-0. Some of the most commonly used wheel arrangements have a type name. For example a locomotive of the 4-6-2 type is known as a Pacific. Some of the most familiar British types illustrated in this book are shown here:

2-2-2	—
2-4-0	—
4-2-2	—
4-4-0	—
4-4-2	'Atlantic'
4-6-0	—
4-6-2	'Pacific'
2-6-0	'Mogul'
2-6-2	'Prairie'
2-8-2	'Mikado'
2-8-0	'Consolidation'
4-6-4	'Baltic'
2-6-0+0-6-2	'Beyer-Garratt'

The following are some common British types almost entirely confined to tank engines:

0-4-4	
0-6-2	
0-6-4	

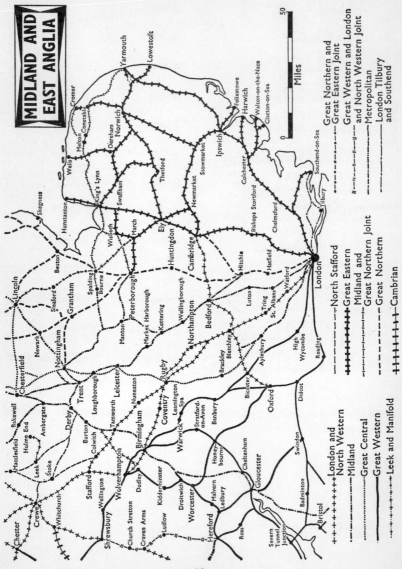

MIDLAND AND EAST ANGLIA

Miles
0 50

London and North Western ++++++++
Midland ————
Great Central ················
Great Western ————
Leek and Manifold +‒+‒+‒+‒+

North Stafford — · — · —
Great Eastern ++++++++
Midland and Great Northern Joint —‒‒—
Great Northern — — —
Cambrian ++++++++

Great Northern and Great Eastern Joint ·•·•·•·
Great Western and London and North Western Joint ‒‖‒‖‒‖‒
Metropolitan ················
London Tilbury and Southend ‒‒‒‒‒‒

INDEX

Midland Railway (*cont.*)	A Johnson 'Belpaire'	92	62	147
	A Deeley compound	110	71	145
	Fowler 'Class 2' 4-4-0	121	77	159
	Lickey banker	145	89	168
Midland and Great Northern Joint	4-4-0 of 1908	86	59	145
North British Railway	Tay Bridge engine	31	32	124
	Drummond 4-4-0	42	37	128
	Holmes 4-4-0	55	44	133
	A Reid Atlantic	106	69	153
	'Glen' class 4-4-0	134	83	164
North Eastern Railway	Long-boilered goods	15	24	118
	Fletcher '901' 2-4-0	32	32	124
	4-2-2 Compound	59	46	135
	4-4-0 'Rail-Crusher'	65	49	137
	'R' class 4-4-0	82	57	143
	Class 'X' shunter	118	75	157
	'Z' class 4-4-2	124	78	160
	'T2' class 0-8-0	139	86	166
	The Raven 4-6-2	154	93	171
North London Railway	4-4-0 T (green)	35	34	126
	Adams 4-4-0 T	53	43	132
North Staffordshire Railway	Adams 4-4-2 T	114	73	156
	Hookhams 0-6-4 T	138	85	165
Rhymney Railway	0-6-2 tank 1909	77	55	142
Romney Hythe and Dymchurch Railway	15-inch gauge 4-8-2	182	107	182
Snowdon Mountain Railway	Swiss rack engine	90	61	147
Somerset and Dorset Joint Railway	4-4-0 of 1903	85	59	145
	2-8-0 of 1914	135	84	164
Southern Railway	'King Arthur' 4-6-0	155	94	172
	'Lord Nelson' 4-6-0	159	96	173
	'Schools' class 4-4-0	168	100	177
	'Merchant Navy' 4-6-2	183	108	183
Sohut Eastern Railway	Sharp 2-2-2	9	21	116
	Cudworth mail 2-2-2	18	25	119
	Stirling 'F' 4-4-0	50	41	131
South Eastern and Chatham Railway	'E' class 4-4-0	108	70	154
	'N' class 2-6-0	142	87	167
	Maunsell 'E1' class	143	88	167
Stockton and Darlington	The *Locomotion*	1	17	113
	The *Derwent*	4	18	114
Taff Vale Railway	Riches 0-6-2 T	75	54	141
Talyllyn Railway	Original engine of 1865	180	106	182
Vale of Rheidol	2-6-2 tank (1923)	179	106	181

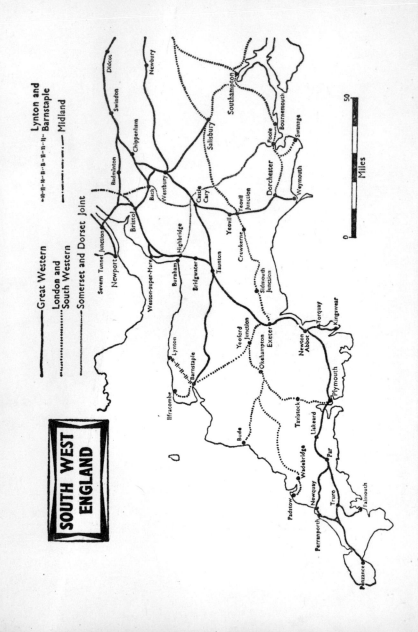

SOUTH WEST ENGLAND

Great Western
London and South Western
Somerset and Dorset Joint
Lynton and Barnstaple
Midland

Miles
0   50

Severn Tunnel Junction
Newport
Bristol
Weston-super-Mare
Burnham
Highbridge
Bridgwater
Taunton
Badminton
Bath
Westbury
Chippenham
Swindon
Didcot
Newbury
Southampton
Salisbury
Castle Cary
Yeovil
Yeovil Junction
Crewkerne
Poole
Bournemouth
Swanage
Dorchester
Weymouth
Sidmouth Junction
Yeoford Junction
Exeter
Okehampton
Newton Abbot
Torquay
Kingswear
Plymouth
Liskeard
Par
Tavistock
Bude
Wadebridge
Padstow
Perranporth
Newquay
Truro
Falmouth
Penzance
Lynton
Barnstaple
Ilfracombe